A FOODIE'S
London

OVER 100 OF THE CAPITAL'S FINEST FOOD SHOPS AND EXPERIENCES

miso burnt aubergine
pickled Jerusalem artichoke
and jalapeño sauce
Pea and mint croquette
with mange tout
salad and paprika yoghurt
Cured mackerel with pickled
vegetables, broad bean salad
confit garlic yoghurt
Ricotta and basil stuffed
courgette
Monday to
Thursday to
Sunday
Small salad
Large salad
Cheese Straw
Granola Bar
Cheese and Chard pie

A FOODIE'S GUIDE TO
London

OVER 100 OF THE CAPITAL'S FINEST FOOD SHOPS AND EXPERIENCES

CARA FROST-SHARRATT

Read. Learn. Do What You Love.

Originally published by New Holland Publishers (UK) Ltd

Published 2015—IMM Lifestyle Books

www.IMMLifestyleBooks.com

IMM Lifestyle Books are distributed in the UK by Grantham Book Service.

In North America, IMM Lifestyle Books are distributed by

Fox Chapel Publishing

1970 Broad Street

East Petersburg, PA 17520

www.FoxChapelPublishing.com

ISBN 978 1 5048 0009 9

Printed in the United States of America

10 9 8 7 6 5 4 3 2 1

CONTENTS

INTRODUCTION

The fall and rise of the independent food shop

The independent food shop has travelled a rocky road over the last hundred years or so. Food shopping was always traditionally done in a number of specific shops, usually on a daily basis. But the rise of the supermarket and the evolution of the family unit gradually led to less time being available for, and allocated to, choosing and buying food. As more families included two working adults, or single working parents, people generally had less time to plan meals, go out shopping and cook time-consuming dishes. Suppertime was no longer set in stone; it became a transient or moveable feast, often dictated not by the time dinner was ready but by when family members were around to eat it. The

loss of the dinner table and the flexibility and convenience of the microwave, supermarket and takeaway led to the demise of many small, specialist food shops. Where once every high street had a fishmonger, a baker and probably more than one grocer and butcher, it became more commonplace to find a couple of chain cafes and a convenience supermarket. However, we shouldn't despair; the independents are busy making a comeback and Londoners are showing their appreciation with their shopping baskets. Once people have enjoyed the exceptional quality and diversity of the food on offer in independent delis, butchers, bakers etc, it is difficult to return to the more anodyne supermarket shop.

Feel-good food

Buying food from specialist shops makes the whole experience more meaningful. Good food nourishes the body but good food shopping will also nourish the soul. If you indulge yourself by spending ten minutes discussing particular cuts of meat with your butcher, or trying a number of farmhouse cheeses before you pick your favourite, you instantly make that food more special and you become a more discerning and appreciative consumer. You are more connected to the food that you buy; you are aware of where it has come from and the time, effort and dedication that has gone into producing it. You haven't simply picked something from a shelf based on its packaging, its price or its basic usefulness; you have made a conscious decision to choose and buy

food that has aroused your senses. You have sought out specific food based on certain credentials and whether this comes down to ethics, flavour, diversity, provenance, customer service, or the overall experience of talking to and buying from specialist purveyors, you have transformed food shopping from an essential chore into a pleasurable pastime.

Culinary hotspots

London is lucky to have a wide range and choice of specialist shops spread out over the whole of the city but whilst researching this book, I discovered certain roads and areas with a disproportionate number of top-notch food emporiums. It's the old adage of like attracting like and once a brave independent has trail blazed a path, success means it's easier and less risky for others to follow suit.

Gentrification can also lead to clusters of new gourmet-inclined residents following each other to desirable locations. This creates an instant receptive customer base and the cycle of increased amenities and regular custom continues. Once a street or area becomes known for its food shops, people will travel from further afield to avail of this foodie enclave. Lordship Lane in East Dulwich offers a whole road of fantastic independent food shops (many of which you'll find in this book), whilst Royal Hill in Greenwich includes a gorgeous row of fine gourmet emporiums, tucked away from the tourist mayhem of the centre of town. Marylebone High Street is another great foodie destination, as is Northcote Road in Clapham, where you can do a proper old-fashioned grocery shop in the butcher, bakery, fish stall, cheesemonger and wine

merchant. Portobello Road and many of its side streets are worth setting aside time to explore, whilst Borough Market and its immediate environs are on every food lover's map. However, I've realised that you don't have to walk too far from any tube or train station in central London to discover an exciting food purveyor.

Choosing the shops

It is no small task trying to pick the best food shops in London and when faced with it, I felt a bit daunted at the huge amount of research that lay ahead. With the burgeoning independent food scene in the capital, there is now a wealth of top-quality shops in every niche of the food and drink industry, selling carefully sourced groceries, the tastiest seasonal produce, the most beautiful artisan bread, the freshest fish and meat, the finest wine and the most delicious farmhouse cheeses. So, how to go about

narrowing down this impressive selection of food emporiums? The answer is walking.... and miles of it. I explored every part of central London, following up leads and recommendations, re-visiting favourite foodie destinations and chancing upon new ones, narrowing down my shortlist until I had the definitive collection of what I consider to be the best food shops in the capital.

The shops in the book are not all necessarily the biggest in their category; they might not even all have the widest selection of products. But they all have something special, that extra je ne sais quoi that gives you a warm glow inside and makes you walk out feeling happy. They might be quirky, beautiful, stock unique or specialist products, or go above and beyond the call of duty when it comes to service. If you have the same experiences that I did, the staff will be able to tell you exactly where each cheese, bottle of wine or fillet steak comes from,

they will take the time to stop for a chat and they will genuinely appreciate your custom. Some are more than shops alone: they have a cafe or restaurant attached, they run courses, tasting evenings or foodie book clubs, they offer free local delivery or they're active in the local community.

Some of the shops are well known and some you may never have heard of but I hope you get as excited about discovering them as I was. I should point out that this book is very much a subjective work. Whilst there are certain shops with famous names and fine reputations, none have been included purely on the basis of their reputation; they have all earned their place here. I have visited each and every shop and market in the book, wearing out shoes and getting through numerous notebooks on my travels. I've discovered new areas of London, fallen back in love with old haunts and met the most amazing people in the process.

The dedication and commitment shown by the shop owners, managers and staff is extraordinary; these are the people pioneering the independent food revolution in London and you can support them by voting with your feet.

Using the book

To keep things simple, the book is divided by shop type, with entries in each chapter listed in alphabetical order. Most of the shops are located in zones 1 and 2, with a few special exceptions a little further out. By keeping it central, and concentrating on shops that are easy to get to and easy to find, you can discover the best on offer without having to travel too far. There's a box at the end of each entry with suggestions for other shops and food-related amenities close by, so you can better plan your time and also so you don't miss out on anything else in the immediate vicinity.

BAKERIES

Whether you are looking for a loaf of bread to take home, a place to stop for a coffee and a slice of cake, or perhaps an indulgent treat for a special occasion, you can guarantee that London has a bakery to suit. From north to south and east to west, London's bakeries are unbeatable in terms of quality and diversity. Be it a quick stop at the Breadstall in Clapham (see page 12), a mid-shop lunch break at the Exeter Street Bakery in Kensington (see page 20) or a full blow-out at Konditor & Cook near Waterloo (see page 23), there's a bakery in the capital to suit all occasions, tastes and budgets.

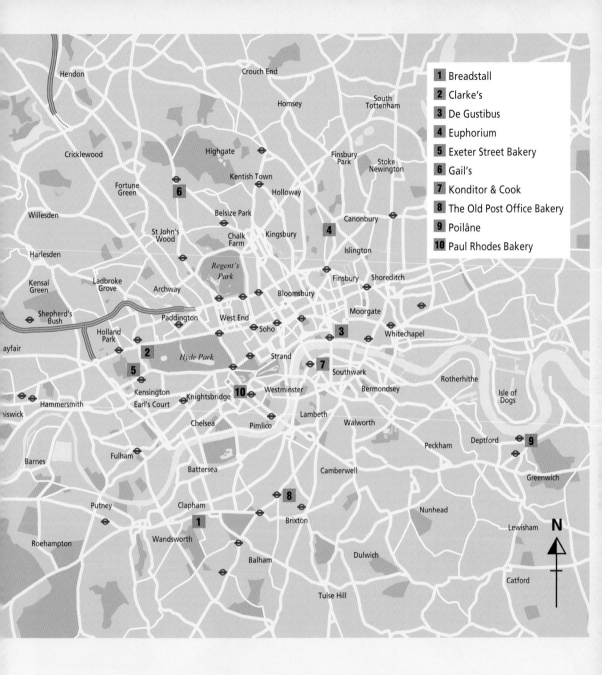

1	Breadstall
2	Clarke's
3	De Gustibus
4	Euphorium
5	Exeter Street Bakery
6	Gail's
7	Konditor & Cook
8	The Old Post Office Bakery
9	Poilâne
10	Paul Rhodes Bakery

Breadstall

60 Northcote Road, London SW11 1PA
Tel: 07966 916760
Opening times: Mon–Sun 8am–6pm
Train: Clapham Junction

Breadstall is like the Winnebago of food stalls. This double-length trailer pays homage to baking and is a permanent fixture on the bustling Northcote Road, providing locals with yet another very good reason to open their wallets. Already spoilt for choice when it comes to independent food purveyors, residents are only too aware that they have lucked out by living here. You'll appreciate the glorious smell of freshly baked bread and cakes long before you see the stall itself. By the time you reach it, you have little choice but to stop whether you are intending to or not. By stopping however, you'll do your taste buds one huge favour.

The display is a feast for all the senses and the range is incredible when you consider that most of the sandwiches and hot foods are made fresh on site daily. Raw ingredients are sourced from Italy and all the other baked goods are freshly made and delivered each morning from 12 different independent bakeries. Why so many? Well, that's down to the fastidious desire for perfection on behalf of the owner Sebastian Vince. Having left a fast-paced career in advertising to set up the business, he has worked hard to stock his stall with the absolute best of everything. So, cupcakes come from one bakery, sausage rolls from another and so on. And with over 600 sausage rolls exchanging hands over the course of a weekend, it's hardly surprising that so many bakeries are needed to stock Breadstall.

While you're in the area...

The list is endless for Northcote Road: Hamish Johnston the cheesemonger (page 52) is a close neighbour and it's a quick step across the road to Dove & Son (page 32) for quality meat. Philglas & Swiggot (page 165) is a lovely independent wine merchant and La Cuisiniere stocks fabulous kitchenware.

Clarke's

122 Kensington Church Street, London W8 4BH
Tel: 020 7229 2190
Opening times: Mon–Fri 8am–8pm, Sat 8am–4pm,
Sun 10am–4pm
Tube: Notting Hill Gate

No detail has been overlooked in this achingly beautiful shop just off the main drag of Notting Hill Gate. Here, you can escape from the tourists and commuters into a calm and elegant space that has been devoted to good food. From the baskets of bread that peep out of the window to the chequered, tiled floor and the dark wooden counter laden down with sandwiches, tarts and quiches to take away, this is a lovely bolthole in which to indulge your artisan food habit. A vast antique dresser is neatly stacked with honey, jam and jelly, neat little cellophane packets of biscuits, brownies and brittle, as well as Monmouth coffee, Umbrian lentils and spelt flour. A chilled counter shows off an impressive selection of fresh filled pasta, terrines and prepared meals while a couple of tables are tucked away at the back for anyone who wishes to stay and soak up the atmosphere while devouring their purchases.

The highly regarded Clarke's restaurant is next-door to the shop. Owner, Sally Clarke, opened it in 1984, with the shop and bakery following a few years later and the businesses work in perfect harmony with each other. The bakery now supplies a huge number of restaurants and shops around the capital, as well as keeping & Clarke's stocked with a constant supply of freshly baked loaves, from brioche to walnut and raisin, and Stilton bread. All the food you see here is baked on site daily using fresh ingredients and seasonal celebrations see the shelves groan under the weight of speciality foods and ingredients, including homemade Stollen, Easter eggs and turkey stuffing.

While you're in the area...

Chegworth Farm Shop (page 147) is just across the road and is packed full of fresh organic goodies. James Knight (page 99) is the place to buy gleaming fresh fish and a wide variety of seafood and it's just a few minutes' walk away on Notting Hill Gate. The Cupcake Company is a den of sugary treats and is just a few doors along from the bakery.

De Gustibus

53-55 Carter Lane, London EC4V 5AE
Tel: 020 7236 0056
Opening times: Mon–Fri 7am-5pm, Sat–Sun closed
Tube: St Paul's

When Dan and Annette started their baking business from their home in Oxfordshire in 1990, most Londoners were used to having their sandwich fillings slapped between two anaemic slices of days-old white bread. Whilst some people still hand over their hard-earned cash for the food equivalent of cardboard, savvy City workers make a beeline for De Gustibus. Over the intervening years, this artisan bakery has become synonymous with exceptional bread, cakes and biscuits and the original bakery in Abingdon, Oxfordshire, still supplies the shops with a dizzying array of freshly baked bread every single day.

'Fresh' is the buzzword here and the spacious, light-filled shop is like an exhibition of bread styles, with loaves lining the inside of the serving counter and filling the stunning window display. People travel here daily from all over the City and beyond for the legendary sourdough and the surprisingly soft and supple 100% rye bread but the choices are endless: there's a subtle roast onion loaf, sun-dried tomato and olive oil bread, a lovely light pumpernickel style bread made with crushed caraway, and sweet raisin, date and walnut bread (the list goes on). You can either buy the additive-free loaves whole, or queue up and choose your bread and filling for the best sandwich you'll ever taste. As with the bread, all the fillings are made fresh every day and, when I visited, the specials included British Bangers, and Indian Kofta. But the bestsellers remain the outstanding slow-cooked pork belly, and home-cured salt beef, which they brine themselves.

Other London branches

4 Southwark Street, London SE1 1TQ

While you're in the area...

If you're looking for top-quality meat, Porterford (page 41) is just a couple of minutes walk east, on Watling Street. Alternatively, cross over Southwark Bridge and take a tasting tour at Vinopolis or check out Borough Market (page 126) and the numerous food shops that surround it like Neal's Yard Dairy (page 54) and Monmouth Coffee.

Euphorium

202 Upper Street, London N1 1RQ
Tel: 020 7704 6905
Opening times: Mon–Fri 7am–10pm,
Sat-Sun 8am–10pm
Tube: Highbury & Islington

the best of British baking

The Upper Street branch of this renowned bakery was the first to open and six more shops around London have since followed it. The emphasis here is on seasonal, local, organic ingredients and although plenty of other food producers use these as buzzwords for their business, the proof is quite literally in the pudding at Euphorium. Freshly baked loaves and pastries are dispatched from the downstairs bakery to this and all the other shops every morning and the smell is simply intoxicating.

The window display is laden with loaves and more are piled in neat little stacks behind the counter, with classic varieties such as organic granary and paysan, along with others like pain de campagne, pain blanc and black olive bread. A 'bread of the day' adds even more choice; on the day I visited, it was Apple and Spice Brioche. Whilst the emphasis is on bread, there is so much more besides, from sourdough and focaccia sandwiches, to pizza slices, bagels, croissants and cakes.

Whether you just come in for your daily bread, or you linger for a coffee and pastry, there's a genuine community feel here, so far removed from the characterless atmosphere of many of the café-by-numbers chains. The food is fresh and inviting, the bread is a joy to devour and the staff look like they're having fun.

Other London branches:

79 Upper Street, London N1 0NU
26a Chapel Market, London N1 9EN
211 Haverstock Hill, London NW3 4QN
45 Southend Road, London NW3 2QB
Thomas Neal's Centre, 35 Earlham Street, London WC2H 9LD
Whiteleys Shopping Centre, 144 Queensway, London W2 6LY

While you're in the area...

Try out some of the many wines that are on tap to taste at The Sampler (page 167), which is just across the road. Next, you can indulge your sweet tooth at Paul A. Young (page 68) in cutesy Camden Passage. Finally, head to Ottolenghi (page 84), where you can choose some tasty sweet and savoury take out.

Exeter Street Bakery

1b Argyll Road, London W8 7DB
Tel: 020 7937 8484
Opening times: Mon–Sat 8am–7pm, Sun 9am–6pm
Tube: High Street Kensington

This bright, airy bakery and café is just a short stroll away from the crazy high-end consumerism of High Street Kensington and it provides the perfect hideaway if you're looking for a quiet spot to brace yourself for, or recover from, a hectic shopping spree. The spotless stainless steel counter shows off the impressive selection of pizzas and flatbreads that are made on site every day, whilst the vast range of fresh loaves are baked in the main bakery in Northwest London and delivered to the shop, still warm from the ovens. Exeter Street also sells its bread at food markets and at top-end outlets all around the capital.

A seated counter space wraps around the large windows and from here you have the perfect vantage point to watch the pizzas being created from scratch in the open kitchen. I'd recommend trying mushroom or salami, or keep it simple with a slice of tomato or margherita pizza. The sandwiches are also made daily and the choice ranges from asparagus to prosciutto. Homemade biscotti, grissini, olive biscuits and delights like rosemary shortbread can be purchased to take away and, whatever you do, don't leave without trying the coffee – it's very good.

While you're in the area...

Satiate your sweet tooth at Hotel Chocolat (page 66) on High Street Kensington, or pop into Carluccio's on the same road for some classy Italian ingredients. Keep walking towards Kensington Road and you'll come across the incredible Whole Foods Market (page 120), a vast emporium of natural and organic goodies. If you want to head back towards Notting Hill, stop off at & Clarke's (page 15) and Chegworth Farm Shop (page 147) on your way.

olio
extra
vergine
d'oliva

ORSO

750 ml

biscuit
£1.20

Gail's

64 Hampstead High Street, London NW3 1QH
Tel: 020 7794 5700
Opening times: Mon–Fri 7am–8pm, Sat 7.30am–8pm,
Sun 8am–8pm
Tube: Hampstead

With a prime spot on chichi Hampstead High Street, it would seem unlikely that a decent bakery and café could fail to attract the paying public. But the locals have discerning taste and will accept nothing short of perfection on the coffee, bread and cake front. Consistently high quality is the key to earning the loyalty and repeat custom of residents around here and Gail's is certainly consistent.

The Hampstead shop is the original branch and successive openings around town are testament to the quality products that are produced here. The bread has fired up the tastebuds of Londoners and Gail's prides itself on its freshly baked loaves that take their inspiration from all over the world. I saw baguettes, French dark sourdough, spelt bread, white sourdough and mixed olive bread stacked up along the bread counter and these are all baked fresh every day. The preservative-free bread is hand-kneaded and slow-fermented to achieve the ultimate in flavour and quality and Gail's is intent on creating a bread revolution in the capital, one customer at a time.

As well as buying whole loaves to devour at home, you can make yourself comfy and indulge in a coffee and pastry, or a hot snack in the café. Personally, I can't get enough of the empanadas and the decadent chocolate pecan brownies, which are totally justified after a lengthy stroll on the heath. Despite its numerous branches, Gail's has managed to maintain a truly local feel with a rare individuality in each of its bakeries. Bread might be a staple food but the loaves here make it so much more than simple sustenance.

Other London branches
64 Northcote Road, London SW11 6QL
282 Chiswick High Road, London W4 1PA
33-35 Exmouth Market, London EC1R 4QL
138 Portobello Road, London W11 2DZ
75 Salusbury Road, London NW6 6NH
5 Circus Road, London NW8 6NX

While you're in the area...
Pure Fruit is a lovely local greengrocers just across the road from Gail's. It is stocked full of fresh, seasonal fruit and vegetables, perfect for filling up the picnic basket ready for a lazy day on Hampstead Heath.

Konditor & Cook

22 Cornwall Road, London SE1 8TW
Tel: 020 7261 0456
Opening times: Mon–Fri 7.30am–6.30pm, Sat 8.30am–3pm, Sun closed
Train/Tube: Waterloo

This branch of the much-loved London bakery is by no means the biggest or the most luxuriously decked out. In fact, it's quite a low-key affair, tucked away down a side street close to Waterloo station. But that's part of its charm. New branches have been springing up all over London to great acclaim and yet this original shop has remained gloriously unfazed by its rise to fame and continues to serve a steady stream of people in the know. Around the quieter residential streets in Waterloo (yes there are some)

it is possibly the worst-kept culinary secret, as locals clamour for the poetic sounding cakes and pastries, the smell of which waft continuously from the front door. And yet, it is so firmly off the beaten track that hapless tourists will indeed feel like they've discovered a hidden gem should they chance upon it while trying to make sense of their A–Z. The lush, plum-coloured shop front has a delightful Dickensian feel and its corner plot allows for a decadent double window display of sweet and

savoury treats. There are whole pies and cakes, and neatly packaged bags of sweet bites and nibbles tied up with ribbon, whilst inside the slices and individual cakes are ready for inspection for sweet-toothed customers.

It's no easy task to choose between Black Gingerbread, Whiskey Bomb and Lemon Crunch Cake but the staff understand such dilemmas and they're happy to let you browse to your heart's content. To make things easier, the coffee menu is refreshingly unpretentious, allowing the food to take centre stage. But it's still top-notch, with a lovely subtle nutty flavour. When I'm in the area, I make a detour to Konditor & Cook simply for a caffeine hit but it would be unthinkable to leave without a cake or two.

Other London branches
63 Stamford Street, London SE1 9NB
10 Stoney Street, London SE1 9AD (Borough Market)
46 Grays Inn Road, London WC1X 8LR
30 St Mary Axe, London EC3A 8BF
Curzon Cinema, Shaftsbury Avenue, London W1D 5DY

While you're in the area...
If you take a short walk across Waterloo Road and onto Lower Marsh you'll be rewarded with a fantastic food shopping experience. Greensmiths (page 108) is one large shop that is home to a butcher (The Ginger Pig), a wine merchant (Waterloo Wine Company), a bakery (The Old Post Office Bakery) and a greengrocer (Solstice). What more do you need?

The Old Post Office Bakery

76 Landor Road, London SW9 9PH
Tel: 020 7326 4408
Opening times: Mon–Sat 7am–6pm, Sun 7am–2pm
Tube: Clapham North

This tiny shop is tucked away on a largely residential street that isn't exactly a hub of gastronomy and yet the bakery has managed to hold its own and endear itself to the local residents and bread lovers from further afield. The miniature space feels crowded with two customers but the palpable warmth from the freshly baked loaves ensures you're cosy, rather than cramped. As we all know, the best things often come in small packages and The Old Post Office Bakery is producing some of the best bread in the capital.

Although busy baking, the genial co-owner Richard took time out to show me around the bustling bakery that extends over three floors behind the shop. It's obvious that this wasn't a purpose-built affair, but each room has adapted to its function perfectly and the whole is both charming and enterprising. The mixer is close to being eligible for a telegram from the Queen but it still produces batch after batch of the shop's trademark organic bread, including rye, pain au levain, wholewheat, onion, soda bread, and holsteiner. The bakers start work early to ensure the shelves are stocked with a variety of freshly baked loaves by opening time. At the weekend there's even more activity, as the team bake extra loaves to sell at various farmers' markets around the city. A range of homemade croissants, cakes and pastries complements the bread range and I tucked into a spectacular slice of Apple and Almond Cake while I made my way back to the tube.

Other London branches:

Greensmiths, 27 Lower Marsh, London SE1 7RG

While you're in the area...

There's not exactly a plethora of shopping facilities close by but if you're up for a stroll, you can reach Clapham Common in about 15 minutes where you should check out M. Moen (page 38), one of the best butchers in town. Afterwards, head to the wonderful patisserie next door for a well-earned rest accompanied by coffee and cake.

Poilâne

46 Elizabeth Street, London SW1W 9PA
Tel: 020 7808 4910
Opening times: Mon–Fri 7.30am–7pm,
Sat 7.30am–6pm
Tube: Sloane Square

This traditional bakery brings a little bit of France to the centre of London. Four bakers work around the clock in the downstairs kitchen to ensure the shelves in the bijou shop are constantly stacked with fresh loaves. The bread is cooked in wood-fired ovens in exactly the same way it was when Pierre Poilâne opened his first shop in Paris in 1932. Sourdough is used as a starter for all the handmade loaves here and it's this large, impressive loaf that the bakery is still renowned for. For my money, it's one of the best sourdoughs you're likely to find in the capital and, as the price of this bread is calculated by weight (others are sold by the loaf), you can choose to buy anything from a single slice to a whole sourdough.

The shop is small and simply furnished with everything revolving around the bread and this pared-down, unfussy philosophy extends to the product range, which is kept intentionally limited to ensure perfection and consistent quality. Each variety has been carefully chosen and there's nothing superfluous or faddy here: the loaves are obviously a labour of love and respect is given to the origin of the recipes and the important role that bread has played throughout history. Whilst I would encourage you to try the sourdough, other loaves such as rye bread, pain de campagne and milk bread are also worthy of your attention.

While you're in the area...

Jeroboams wine merchant (page 161) is a few shops further down the road. If you feel like a high-end cocoa hit, walk back onto Ebury Street and pop into William Curley (page 72) for some of the best patisserie in town. The gorgeous Peggy Porschen Cakes is also on Ebury Street, or, if you want to travel from chocolate to cheese heaven in under ten minutes, check out Rippon Cheese Stores (page 58) on Upper Tachbrook Street.

Paul Rhodes Bakery

37 King William Walk, London SE10 9HU
Tel: 020 8858 8995
Opening times: Mon–Sun 7am-7pm
Train station: Greenwich or Cutty Sark DLR

Business has been booming for this artisan bakery and the man behind the bread dough, Paul Rhodes, has been busy building his empire around town. However, the small but perfectly formed central Greenwich shop was the pioneering permanent base for a bakery that originally earned its reputation in Borough Market. There's a huge range of bread, pastries and cakes but only the seriously focused will be able to walk out with no more than a warm granary loaf under their arm. The chocolate brownies are the stuff of legend in this part of town (and deservedly so, I can confirm), whilst the sandwiches and filled baguettes look almost too good to eat...almost.

Every loaf of bread is lovingly shaped by hand, a slow and laborious process but one that ensures the best results and here, only the best will do. The loaves behind the groaning counter have a truly international feel with Irish soda bread lined up neatly next to focaccia and brioche. The shop is perched on a corner next to the bustling Greenwich indoor market. Locals pop in for their daily fix of freshly baked bread, whilst the weekend sees queues out the door as hungry tourists follow their noses and dutifully line up to buy the best sandwiches, snacks and cakes in Greenwich. A lucky few take advantage of the limited number of barstools and tiny counter space, where purchases can be enjoyed with a freshly brewed Fairtrade coffee. How so many good things can be crammed into such a bijou space beggars belief but this tardis of a bakery is a genuine foodie gem.

Other London braches
26 Notting Hill Gate, London W11 3HY

While you're in the area...
Don't miss The Fishmonger Ltd, The Creaky Shed, The Cheeseboard (page 51) and Drings (page 33), which are all just a short walk away on Royal Hill. There's also a good selection of international food stalls in the market at the weekend.

BUTCHERS

There's something rather wonderful about finding a good local butcher, and on the following pages you'll find recommendations for some of the best butchers in London. You can be assured that the establishments listed here sell good quality meat and that the staff are knowledgeable and helpful. Be it bangers for the barbecue, a joint for the Sunday roast or an extra special treat for a big occasion, these are the people who will help you to make the most out of your purchase.

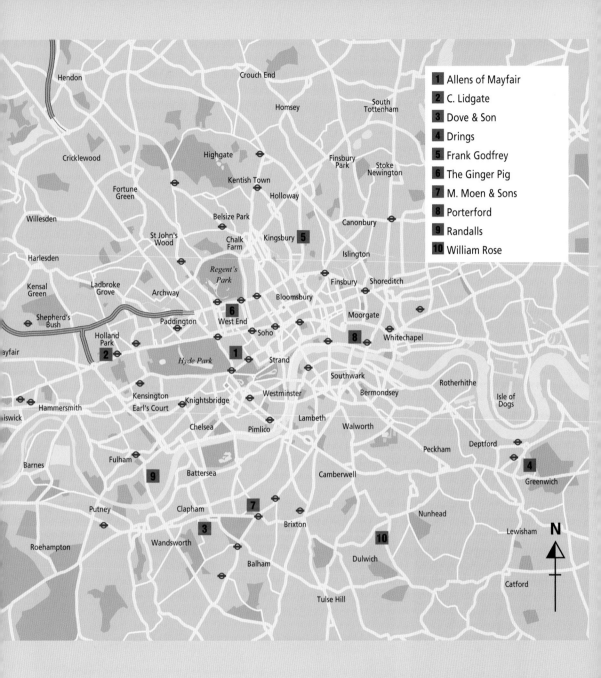

1 Allens of Mayfair
2 C. Lidgate
3 Dove & Son
4 Drings
5 Frank Godfrey
6 The Ginger Pig
7 M. Moen & Sons
8 Porterford
9 Randalls
10 William Rose

Hendon
Crouch End
Homsey
South Tottenham
Cricklewood
Highgate
Finsbury Park
Stoke Newington
Kentish Town
Fortune Green
Holloway
Willesden
Belsize Park
Canonbury
St John's Wood
Chalk Farm
Kingsbury **5**
Harlesden
Islington
Kensal Green
Ladbroke Grove
Archway
Regent's Park
Finsbury
Shoreditch
Shepherd's Bush
Paddington
West End
6
Bloomsbury
Moorgate
Holland Park
2
Soho
8
Whitechapel
ayfair
1
Strand
Hyde Park
Southwark
Rotherhithe
Kensington
Knightsbridge
Westminster
Bermondsey
Isle of Dogs
Earl's Court
Hammersmith
iswick
Chelsea
Pimlico
Lambeth
Walworth
Peckham
Deptford
Barnes
Fulham
Battersea
Camberwell
4
Greenwich
9
Nunhead
Lewisham
Putney
Clapham
7
Brixton
3
Wandsworth
10
Dulwich
Roehampton
Balham
Catford
Tulse Hill

N

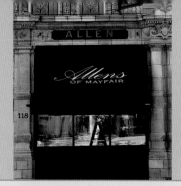

Allens of Mayfair

117 Mount Street, London W1K 3LA
Tel: 020 7499 5831
Opening times: Mon–Fri 7am–5.30pm,
Sat 7am–1.30pm
Tube: Bond Street or Green Park

Allens is a picture postcard butchers. Entering this beautifully appointed shop in the heart of Mayfair is like taking a step back in time. The oversized butchers block is the centrepiece of the space, with ornate Victorian wall tiles offering a complementary backdrop to the utilitarian tools of the trade. Allens prides itself on the quality of its produce and great sides of beef hang impressively above the counters, along with beautiful game birds when they're in season. This visual nod to, and respect for, the animals that are butchered and sold here has been a feature of the shop for its entire 120 years of existence. It elevates the art of butchery and reminds customers why they choose to buy their meat here, rather than from a chilled supermarket cabinet.

The longevity of Allens speaks volumes about the consistently fine food that it sources and sells. The current owners have worked hard to make it a name that is respected by restaurateurs and the general public alike. There's even the opportunity to go beyond the usual shopping experience of buying your chops ready chopped. Beginner's butchery courses allow you to learn the secrets of good butchery and to prepare a box of your own cut meat. And if you don't call London home, there's a comprehensive online ordering and delivery service that allows the abundance of good things in the Mount Street shop to be enjoyed anywhere in the UK.

While you're in the area...

The Mount Street Deli is just a few doors away at number 100. This lavishly appointed little shop is ideal for a posh pit stop. A daily menu of gorgeous salads and sandwiches uses the best of British and Italian ingredients.

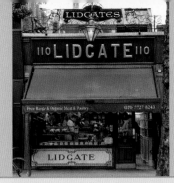

C. Lidgate

110 Holland Park Avenue, London W11 4UA
Tel: 020 7727 8243
Opening times: Mon–Fri 6.30am–7pm, Sat 6.30am–6.30pm, Sun closed
Tube: Holland Park

David Lidgate is the fourth generation of Lidgates to stand behind the counter and business has been consistent for all of the company's impressive 150 years of trading. It is so well established in the area that everyone from keen home cooks to celebrity chefs and food critics swear by the quality of the meat sold here. The classic looking frontage with its mosaic tiles is an open and friendly affair that allows potential customers to gaze past the beautifully stacked window display to the immense and equally well-appointed counter inside. Here, staff dressed in aprons and boaters serve a constant queue of customers. Once you've seen what's on offer, it's very difficult to walk away empty-handed, whether or not you've got a meat supper planned.

David is extremely fussy when it comes to sourcing the meat and only the best will do. Everything is personally selected from a choice range of organic and free-range farms in England and the meat looks incredibly fresh, vibrant in colour and appetising. In fact, it's one of the best butcher displays you're likely to see on your culinary travels around the capital. There are lamb knuckles, dainty little noisettes, pork ribs and plump pork tenderloins, as well as ossobuco, spatchcock poussin and butterflied lamb legs. There's a select range of homemade sausages and the legendary and award-winning pies that are cooked in ceramic dishes have pie lovers hooked after their first foray. Try Lamb, Leek and Apricot, or play it safe with Steak and Kidney, or the Shepherd's Pie, which will leave you vowing never to cook your own again.

While you're in the area...

Stop off at Maison Blanc for posh tea and cakes, check out the range of fine wines in Jeroboams (page 161) and go round the corner to Clarendon Road for an amazing selection of fresh produce in Michanicou Brothers (page 151).

Dove & Son

71 Northcote Road, London SW11 6PJ
Tel: 020 7223 5191
Opening times: Mon 8am–4pm, Tues–Sat
8am–6pm
Train: Clapham Junction

Bob Dove is a real character and he's the only butcher left in a family that has been running this shop on these premises for 120 years. If you catch him during a quiet time, he'll stand and chat about everything from the supermarkets that threaten the existence of independent food shops, to his fascinating family history. It's precisely this type of warm customer service that distinguishes local traders from the multinational food colossi. Everyone in Dove's has time for a chat. Butchery is a craft and they're so efficient at multitasking, you'll be treated to a verbal essay on the state of the economy or some juicy local retail gossip while your pork chops are being prepared.

This independent family butcher has seen huge changes over the years, not least the demise of all but a few of the other butchers, fishmongers and grocers on Northcote Road. But Bob is proud of his product and believes that if people make the effort to buy from local traders, they'll soon appreciate the quality on offer. Dove's specialises in free-range beef, English lamb and outdoor-reared pork but there's also a freezer packed full of handmade pies, casseroles and soups. In summer, Dove's also doubles up as a gelateria, with ice cream made on the premises in flavours ranging from 'salted caramel swirl' to 'blossom'. A butcher's shop selling homemade ice cream might sound a bit quirky but if you've met Bob Dove you won't be a bit surprised.

While you're in the area...

Northcote road is a treasure trove of foodie finds. Fish lovers can buy fresh fish and seafood from the fish stall, whilst Salumeria Napoli is stocked full of Italian deli favourites. Hamish Johnston (page 52) is a much-loved cheesemonger; Breadstall (page 12) is a one-stop shop for bread, cakes and savoury snacks, and Philglas & Swiggot (page 165) will supply all your wine needs.

Drings

22 Royal Hill, London SE10 8RT
Tel: 020 8858 4032
Opening times: Mon–Sat 8am–5pm,
Thurs 8am–1pm, Sun closed
Train: Greenwich or Greenwich DLR

When brothers David and Robert Dring recently retired, they didn't have to look too far for a new owner for their eminently popular and highly regarded family butchers. Michael Jones already owned The Cheeseboard next door and he gladly took over the business in a smooth transition that has ensured the residents of Royal Hill remain spoilt when it comes to food. Drings sits in a little row of independent food shops that is discreetly tucked away from the relative craziness of touristy Greenwich. Whilst weekend visitors jostle for breathing space in the market, savvy locals quietly queue for top-quality meat in this traditional shop with all the trimmings.

Drings has been charming its clientele since 1910, so it's had plenty of time to build up good customer relations, but the staff go above and beyond the expected call of duty. Even on a busy day, nothing is too much trouble and repeat custom is valued and rewarded with cheerful service and consistently good-quality meat. If you need advice on how to cook a specific cut or what to use for a particular recipe, there's always a reassuring amount of confidence in the answer.

There's a wide range of organic and free-range meat as well as game, when it's in season, and some seriously good sausages that are all prepared on site. If there's something that particularly tickles your taste buds that's not usually stocked in the shop, they'll happily order it for you. Of course, it's around Christmas time that the orders here really pile in and the Drings Christmas Eve queue is a local festive highlight. People arrive from dawn to collect their turkeys and geese but the enormous queue is kept warm and jovial with mulled wine.

While you're in the area...

You don't have to wander too far to get the rest of your shopping. Drings sits in between The Cheeseboard (page 51) and a lovely grocer's called The Creaky Shed. Walk ten paces around the corner to Circus Street and you'll find The Fishmonger Ltd, which manages to cram dozens of varieties of fish and seafood into a tiny space. If you need a caffeine hit, The Greenhouse flower shop has a cute little café area and Buenos Aires is a delicious haven of homemade snacks and quality coffee (both on Royal Hill).

Frank Godfrey

7 Highbury Park, London N5 1QL
Tel: 020 7226 2425
Opening times: Mon–Fri 8am–6pm,
Sat 8am–5pm
Tube: Highbury & Islington or Arsenal

Many shops claim to be 'family businesses' but few have the same credentials as Frank Godfrey. Frank started the company over 100 years ago and today his great-grandsons, Chris, Jeremy and Philip are at the helm. It's little wonder that this particular butcher has remained so popular over the years; when I visited there was a steady stream of customers but the affable and unflappable Chris still took time out to have a chat and show me around the cold store and prep room. The brothers clearly run this successful business on the merits of both its food and its customer service. The displays are crammed full of vibrant, fleshy chops, steaks and mince and the interior is pristine and proudly tended with well-earned awards displayed on the walls.

Chris is keen to return to a more traditional way of butchering and selling meat. Unlike many modern butchers, he buys whole carcasses and breaks them down, ensuring that all parts of the animal are used. That way, he can respond to customer requirements and also put his skills and experience to full use. He's conscious of food miles and tries to buy his meat from farms close to London, but it's all down to quality in the end, which is why he constantly sources his rare breed beef, pork and lamb from different suppliers. The chicken is free range, the sausages are homemade and Chris even makes his own stock and preps root vegetables so customers can buy everything they need for the ultimate 'ready meal'.

While you're in the area...

Highbury Vintners is just down the road and worth checking out for its great range of wines. Walk the other way along Highbury Park, towards Angel, and you'll find Da Mario deli and the wonderful La Fromagerie (page 53). Keep walking and you'll be spoilt for choice on Upper Street with shops like Euphorium bakery (page 19), Ottolenghi (page 84) and The Sampler (page 167) to whet your appetite.

The Ginger Pig

8-10 Moxon Street, London W1U 4EW
Tel: 020 7935 7788
Opening times: Mon–Thurs 9am–6pm,
Fri–Sat 9am-6.30pm, Sun 10am–3pm
Tube: Baker Street

All traditional and all English could be the tagline for this superb Marylebone butchers as this sums the shop up perfectly. If you chat to the staff while they're neatly wrapping your purchases, you'll be struck by the passion they have for their products and the pride taken in selling this fine fare to their devoted customers. The Ginger Pig, which was founded by Tim Wilson, owes its name to the Tamworth pig, one of many traditional breeds of pig, cattle and sheep that are reared on the company's farms in Yorkshire and taken directly to its shops. It is this direct link between farm and counter that has earned The Ginger Pig its fine reputation and ensured its continued success.

The shop itself is delightfully understated, with a classic layout displaying a wide selection of meat cuts, as well as sausages, pies, pates and quiches, all of which are made on site, or at the Yorkshire farms. The pared down interior allows the produce to speak for itself and the counters are permanently stacked with joints and cuts of the highest quality. Comeback cuts such as oxtail, ox cheeks and liver are given equal standing with classic chops and steaks. However, there is more to this butcher than a workaday shop front. The Ginger Pig also offers butchery courses, enabling the general public to acquaint themselves with the delicate art of slicing and dicing pork, lamb and beef.

Other London braches:

Borough Market, London SE1 1TL
99 Lauriston Road, London E9 7HJ
27 Lower March, London SE1 7RG

While you're in the area...

The Marylebone branch of La Fromagerie (page 53) is literally next door and shouldn't be missed. You can also pop into Orrery Epicurie for a spot of breakfast or gaze longingly at the gorgeous kitchenware in Divertimenti (both on Marylebone High Street).

M. Moen & Sons

24 The Pavement, London SW4 0JA
Tel: 020 7622 1624
Opening times: Mon–Fri 8.30am–6.30pm,
Sat 8.30am–5pm
Tube: Clapham Common

Maurice Moen opened his first butcher shop in South Norwood in 1971 and this is a family business, with son Garry now at the helm. A couple of moves saw the shop first relocate to Clapham and, more recently, to its current larger premises. Indeed, size is the first thing that strikes you when you walk inside this traditional shop that has been carefully restored and renovated to recreate the look and feel of a Victorian butcher. There are various counters running along the length and breadth of the large, airy space but there's not a chop or a chicken thigh out of place: everything is beautifully presented and obviously well considered. Garry is a quietly spoken man who cares passionately about his business and the food that he sells. Having spent years building up relationships with suppliers, he is now confident that they appreciate his insistence on quality. His mantra is 'whatever's right at the right time' and if something isn't up to scratch, it simply won't be stocked. As well as seasonal game, free-range chicken and a selection of organic and free-range pork, lamb and beef, there are homemade sausages, meatballs, burgers and biltong, and prepared meat like satay, kofta and chicken Kievs, not to mention the speciality cured and uncured acorn-fed pork.

The move to the larger premises has allowed M. Moen to expand its range of food beyond meat. You'll find fresh, seasonal fruit and vegetables, cheese, pâté and confit, as well as a large grocery section stocked with British and Continental specialities ranging from Spanish paprika and pimentos to old-fashioned brown sauce, anchovy sauce and pickled walnuts.

While you're in the area...

Don't leave without popping into Macaron, which is next door to the butchers. It's a beautiful, traditional French Patisserie. Esca on Clapham High Street is a café-deli that is hard to walk past and MacFarlane's on nearby Abbeville Road is a fromagerie and deli that is world class.

Porterford

72 Watling Street, London EC4M 9BJ
Tel: 020 7248 1396
Opening times: Mon–Thurs 6.30am–6.30pm,
Fri 6am–7.30pm, Sat–Sun closed
Tube: Mansion House

Porterford has been selling quality meat and game to City gents for 28 years. The shop moved a short distance to its current location in 2004 and it really is a little gem in the heart of the City. If you walk here via Queen Victoria Street, you'll enjoy sneaky little peaks of St Paul's Cathedral. It towers over the lunchtime pedestrians snaking their way along Watling Street, many of them ducking into Porterford to buy the makings of dinner. When I visited there was a constant queue of regular patrons but the manager, George Walker, still had time to talk, taking great pride in the quality and selection of meat in the shop. He has every right to be proud, both of the stock and the shop. The meat is carefully displayed against a backdrop of tiled walls and decorative wood features and the staff work quickly and efficiently. Most of the meat is sourced from the UK with aged Scottish beef, Welsh and Devonshire lamb, and seasonal game being particular specialities.

Porterford is one of the last butcher's in the City of London, which must work in their favour in terms of custom but it is also a sad reflection of the way in which work-hassled commuters do their shopping. Having said that, Porterford offers no excuses for swapping the butcher for the supermarket ready meal aisle: there are homemade pies and plenty of prepared meat like chicken Kiev and stuffed duck that can be cooked more quickly than a TV dinner.

While you're in the area...

It's just a five-minute walk back in the direction of St Paul's to the wonderful bakery, De Gustibus

(page 16). Don't worry if you get lost; the smell of freshly baked bread will set you back on course. If you want a longer walk, head towards Liverpool Street and the twin delights of Brick Lane and Spitalfields Market.

Randalls

113 Wandsworth Bridge Road, London SW6 2TE
Tel: 020 7736 3426
Opening times: Mon-Fr 8.30am–5.30pm, Sat
7am–4pm, Sun closed
Tube: Fulham Broadway or Parsons Green

This popular local butcher has ensured a steady stream of customers due to the consistent high quality of all the meat sold here. It's not in a destination shopping area but that only further demonstrates the commitment to serving the local community and supplying the best of the best. Randalls specialises in free range and organic meat, as well as game when it's in season. They source naturally fed meat and everything is from the UK, apart from the veal. There's Somerset lamb and chicken from Norfolk and Essex and there's also a good range of prepared meats, which is the modern butcher's retaliation to the supermarket ready meal. The offerings here are fantastic, with lamb noisettes in redcurrant and rosemary and chicken escalopes looking particularly good when I visited. There's also a range of pies such as chicken and mushroom, and Guinness, steak and onion.

Aside from the meat, Randalls also sells a good range of grocery products and there's a whole dresser dedicated to gorgeous jams, honey, sauces, mustards and chutneys. When you add in the cheese counter with Appleby, Chaumes and Manchego, amongst others, this is a great local shop that has evolved to meet customer needs without losing sight of its original purpose. Good quality meat is at the centre of the business but it's so much more than a butchers.

While you're in the area...

It's a ten-minute walk to the incredible Wimbledon Wine Cellar (page 173) in Chelsea Harbour where you can search through 1,000 bottles of wine for something to go with you meat purchases. A longer walk will take you to Vagabond (page 171) with 100 wines available to taste all the time.

William Rose

126 Lordship Lane, London SE22 8HD
Tel: 020 8693 9191
Opening times: Tues–Sat 8am–5pm
Train: East Dulwich

I f you want a lesson in how to create the perfect window display, this is the shop to visit. It is a thing of beauty with an impeccable arrangement of meat cuts, offal and whole plucked birds and other game. It comes as no great surprise that the staff arrive well before opening time to arrange the display. There's a level of care that sets this independent family business apart from many of its counterparts and more than justifies its place in this book.

William Rose moved from Vauxhall to its current premises in 2005. Having already been established for well over 100 years, it has succeeded in winning over the hearts and wallets of its East Dulwich clientele in no time at all. The shop specialises in seasonal game and rare breeds such as Gloucester Old Spot, Longhorn cattle and wild Scottish venison. Sausages are homemade on site and there's a constantly changing choice, including lamb and game varieties, as well as the ever-popular pork. There's even the opportunity to get your hands on some serious blades by signing up for The Carnivore Club butchery class at the sister shop in East Dulwich Grove. The traditional butchery and customer service at William Rose ensures people eschew the supermarket pre-packs in favour of the in-depth knowledge of the highly trained staff here. The fact that they've opened a second shop just around the corner proves that people want the choice, expertise and consistent quality that a top-notch local butcher provides.

Other London branches

75 East Dulwich Grove, London SE22 8PR

While you're in the area...

You could spend a whole day wandering around the food shops on Lordship Lane. If you like wine, step inside the wonderful shop and bar at Green & Blue (page 160). For top-quality fish and seafood, head to Moxons (page 100), then stock up on fruit and vegetables at Franklins Farm Shop (page 149). The Cheeseblock (page 49) regularly stocks over 250 varieties of cheese, and East Dulwich Deli (page 78) sells just about everything else you could possibly need for a foodie feast.

CHEESEMONGERS

London has a selection of truly splendid cheesemongers selling some of the finest cheeses available. The cheeses you'll find on sale in these establishments are a million miles from the plastic-wrapped varieties you'll find on sale in most supermarkets, and the taste cannot be compared. So why not pop into the famous Neal's Yard Dairy (see page 54) to sample their delicious artisan cheeses, visit the impressive Androuet in Spitalfields (see page 48) or get something really special for the cheeseboard at Hamish Johnston in Clapham (see page 52).

1 Androuet
2 The Cheese Block
3 The Cheeseboard
4 Hamish Johnston
5 La Fromagerie
6 Neal's Yard Dairy
7 Paxton & Whitfield
8 Rippon Cheese Stores

Androuet

107b Commercial Street, London E1 6BG
Tel: 020 7375 3168
Opening time: Mon–Fri 11am–8pm, Sat 11am–7pm,
Sun 10am–7pm
Tube: Liverpool Street or Aldgate

This destination French cheesemonger is worth a detour from practically anywhere in London. As it is, the shop happens to be located in one of the great foodie areas of the capital so there's plenty more reasons to justify a day trip to Spitalfields. The old-fashioned shop front with its olive green colour scheme is wonderfully inviting and it would be hard to pass it by, even if cheese wasn't featured on your shopping list. The simple wood fittings and cheeseboard in the centre of the room make browsing a pleasure. There's no singular glass counter that can make cheese buying a little intimidating for the novice. Here, it's all about getting close to the cheese and not simply staring at it through a glass display.

But enough about the interior décor and layout, let's talk cheese. Androuet has been a respected name in Paris since the beginning of the last century when Henri Androuet opened his first shop. Branches are now dotted around the city of Paris, selling artisan cheeses that have been sourced from small producers and the London shop echoes this

ethos. The list is mainly devoted to France but there are nods to other great cheese producing countries as well. There are classics such as Camembert, Reblochon and Brie, as well as an abundance of lesser-known cow and goats' milk cheeses like Laval and Cantal, one of the oldest French cheeses. The Spitalfields shop opened in 2010 but it's already firmly embedded in the rich and varied food culture of the area. There's also a tiny restaurant that's literally attached to the shop, with bar stools and a menu that offers cheese lovers the chance to combine good cheese with top-end charcouterie and fine wine.

While you're in the area...

Spitalfields Market is one of the best in London and the surrounding shops will tickle your taste buds. Montezuma's (page 67) is in the market hall, whilst the adorable duo of shops, A. Gold (page 144) and Verde & Co. are a few steps away, in the direction of Liverpool Street, and shouldn't be missed. Head back in the other direction and the joys of Brick Lane and Shoreditch await you.

The Cheese Block

69 Lordship Lane, London SE22 8EP
Tel: 020 8299 3636
Opening times: Mon–Fri 9am-7pm, Sat 9am-6pm, Sun 10am–1pm
Train: East Dulwich

The Cheese Block is exactly as a cheesemongers should be: it's all about the cheese and shop life centres around the huge chilled cabinet that regularly contains an astonishing 275 varieties. The cheeses stocked are mainly European with a couple of exceptions. The Cheese Block concentrates on classic and lesser-known varieties from top cheese-producing countries such as France, Spain, Italy, Holland and the UK. There's a smattering of representation from Switzerland and Greece too, to complete the vast and varied selection on offer.

With 19 years of trade on Lordship Lane under its belt, The Cheese Block is no new kid on the block. It was already well established before this south-east London postcode became a favourite with baby boomer foodies looking to upsize but remain within spitting distance of central London. What I love about The Cheese Block is that while the street outside has been transformed, little inside this traditional shop appears to have changed. The owners are simply passionate about cheese and are keen to help people experiment and discover new varieties. They believe there's a specific cheese for every mood and when people come in describing what kind of cheese they want, they are often merely putting their feelings into words. This cheese healing theory was put to the test when I asked for a strong, pungent cheese. The Spanish blue cheese, Cabrales, was the perfect recommendation.

While you're in the area...

You're in a food lover's paradise on Lordship Lane. Make the most of it by buying your fish and seafood in Moxon's (page 100), meat in William Rose (page 45), deli delights in East Dulwich Deli (page 78) and organic groceries in SMBS Foods. Then you can relax with a well-earned glass of wine in Green & Blue (page 160).

The Cheeseboard

26 Royal Hill, London SE10 8RT
Tel: 020 8305 0401
Opening times: Mon–Weds 9am–5pm, Thurs 9am–1pm,
Fri 9am–5.30pm, Sat 9am–5pm, Sun closed
Train: Greenwich or Greenwich DLR

The Cheeseboard forms part of a small but complimentary row of shops that includes a fishmonger, butcher and grocer. This miniature independent high street has a village feel: reusable jute bags are de rigour and bicycles are left unlocked whilst their owners pop in for a wedge of Y-Fenni or a couple of pork chops. You could be forgiven for thinking you'd landed slap bang in the middle of a cutesy Kent village and the shopkeepers seem to be of the same mind. Browsing and tasting is positively encouraged in The Cheeseboard and, despite its diminutive proportions, there's plenty to arouse the taste buds.

The Cheeseboard has been slicing up truckles of Cheddar for 25 years and its reputation has been built on the sound knowledge of all the 100-plus European cheeses that it stocks. You'll find much-loved British classics such as Stinking Bishop and Cornish Yarg along with more unusual varieties from Norway and Spain and everything else in between. If you're looking for something new, this is a great shop in which to broaden your cheese horizons and you'll be expertly guided through the gamut of regional cheeses on offer.

The shop is primarily concerned with cheese but it has also taken on the mantle of provisions store, to ensure that a shopping trip on Royal Hill can genuinely sustain a larder without the need to venture into a supermarket. Freshly baked croissants and a huge range of loaves from bloomers to rye, and soda bread, sit jauntily in the window display. There's milk, juice, yogurt, cheese biscuits and chutneys, as well as a good little

VULSCOMBE
DEVON GOATS CHEESE
£3.95

selection of wine for shoppers who stop by later on in the day and are thinking about dinner.

While you're in the area...

Go next door to Drings (page 33) for equally good customer service, then next door again, to The Creaky Shed, for quality fruit and vegetables. If fish is on the menu, head back around the corner to The Fishmonger Ltd on Circus Street.

Hamish Johnston

48 Northcote Road, London SW11 1PA
Tel: 020 7738 0741
Opening times: Mon–Sat 9am–6pm, Sun 11am–4pm
Train: Clapham Junction

Hamish Johnston completes the complement of independent food retailers on Northcote Road. With a quality fish stall, bakery, butcher and wine merchant on the strip, there's no need to wander within fifty yards of a supermarket for everyday groceries. Of course, just because the need isn't there, the convenience factor can act like a magnet for time poor Londoners, even when such quality and diversity is available in specialist independent shops.

Owners, Will Hamish Johnston and Mark Newman, have successfully weathered the storm of

the food superstores by stocking an exciting selection of artisan British and European cheeses. But it's not just the choice of cheesy treats that attracts customers and keeps them coming back; it's the encyclopaedic knowledge of the staff. There's nothing they don't know about what's behind the counter and, as cheese preferences can be a very personal affair, it's good to have a little proverbial handholding when choosing your cheeseboard. Specialities include creamy Golden Cross and Flower Marie goats' cheeses from East Sussex, Sparkenhoe Red Leicester and the wonderful unpasteurised Stichelton blue cheese. You can expect to be greeted by about 150 varieties any time you visit.

Although cheese is the mainstay of this quaint little corner store with its distinctive turquoise shop front, there's plenty more to tempt shoppers inside. A deli section offers cured meat and smoked salmon, there are shelves of delicious pickles, jellies, pasta, olive oil, fresh eggs and, naturally, mountains of cheese biscuits. Monmouth Coffee and Rococo Chocolates complete the range, making it somewhat of a challenge to leave the shop armed with only a couple of wedges of cheese.

While you're in the area...

There's really no need for recommendations in this part of town. Come out of Hamish Johnston, turn left or right and you'll soon arrive in yet another foodie haven. Dove & Son (page 32), Philglas & Swiggot (page 165), Breadstall (page 12) and Salumeria Napoli are just a few names to look out for. They're all on Northcote Road.

La Fromagerie

30 Highbury Park, London N5 2AA
Tel: 020 7359 7440
Opening times: Mon 10.30am–7pm, Tues–Fri
9am–7pm, Sat 9am–7pm, Sun 10am–5pm
Tube: Holloway Road or Arsenal

If you know your Cheshire from your Cheddar but get a bit flummoxed when it comes to anything more unusual, a cheesemonger can seem both enticing and intimidating. Not so with La Fromagerie. The utter devotion to all things cheese related has seen the company quietly educating novice cheese fiends and nurturing the taste buds of more accustomed palates since 1992, when Patricia and Danny Michelson opened the Highbury shop. It's smaller than its Marylebone counterpart, which opened ten years later, but the ambience in both stores is the same. The cosy interior encourages browsing and the signature dark wood, eclectic décor and baskets of fresh produce and croissants make for some top-quality, feel-good shopping.

This inviting and relaxed form of food shopping in firmly entrenched in the ethos of those working in the independent sector and what better way to make your customers feel welcome than by encouraging them to stay for a drink and a bite to eat? The dinky tasting café in Highbury offers a small but perfectly formed menu of seasonal fare and choice cheeses, whilst the larger Moxon Street shop can accommodate more diners and a bigger menu. When it comes to the main event, there's a dizzying array of wonderful artisan cheeses to choose from. All the cheese is allowed to mature on site, which means that it's only sold once it has reached peak condition. From traditionally produced farmhouse cheeses, such as Gouda with truffles, to seasonal English cheese like the tangy Beenleigh Blue, the enthusiastic staff will take their time finding out exactly what you want.

Other London branches:

2-6 Moxon Street, London W1U 4EW

While you're in the area...

Esteemed butcher Frank Goddfrey (page 35) is just a minute's walk away on Highbury Park and another few minutes' stroll along the same road will find you at the rated local independent wine retailer, Highbury Vintners.

Neal's Yard Dairy

17 Shorts Gardens, London WC2H 9AT
Tel: 020 7240 5700
Opening times: Mon–Sat 10am–7pm, Sun closed
Tube: Covent Garden

This is unarguably the most well-known cheese shop in town but it has a reputation that has been built up on quality as opposed to notoriety. The original shop in Neal's Yard first opened its doors in 1979, selling its own cheese and yogurt. However, it quickly progressed to championing independent cheese makers and the shelves gradually filled up with a vast array of artisan cheeses from diverse producers all over the UK. In 1992 the shop moved to its current location in Shorts Gardens in order to accommodate more cheese and, a few years down the line, a second shop opened in Borough Market. This has even more space, including maturing rooms in railway arches under the London to Dover mainline, which offer the ideal cool and humid conditions for maturing cheese. Here, a team of five people takes care of the cheeses.

Neal's Yard Dairy now works closely with over 70 UK and Irish cheese makers, all producing exceptional cheese. Buyers regularly visit the producers to taste new cheese and this is very much a hands-on operation with the producers and the customers being linked by a team of dedicated cheese lovers. The shop is perennially busy but the staff are never too rushed to offer tasters and advice: what they don't know about the cheese stocked in this dairy den simply isn't worth knowing. You'll find classic blue cheeses like Cashel Blue and Colston Bassett Stilton, a dizzying array of Cheddars and a great selection of goats' cheeses, such as Innes Log and Stawley. There's even Buffalo Mozzarella from Hampshire. If you just can't make up your mind, you can always book a place on one

of the popular cheese tastings at the Borough shop. There's at least one a week, with different themes and cheeses being covered every time.

Other London branches:

6 Park Street, London SE1 9AB

While you're in the area...

Load up on hot drinks and treats at Euphorium Bakery (page 19) in the basement of Thomas Neal's Centre in the heart of Covent Garden. Or simply walk across the yard onto Monmouth Street for one of the best coffees in town, courtesy of Monmouth Coffee. It's then a matter of minutes to both Bill's and Carluccios for a basketful of deli delights.

WESTCOMBE CHEDDAR

TOM CALVER AND RICHARD CALVER
LOWER WESTCOMBE FARM, EVERCREECH,
SOMERSET

RAW MILK
FRIESIAN AND HOLSTEIN COWS
TRAD. ANIMAL RENNET   £20.30

KEEN'S CHEDDAR

JAMES KEEN AND NICK KEEN
MOORHAYES FARM, WINCANTON, SOMERSET

RAW MILK
HOLSTEIN COWS
TRAD. ANIMAL RENNET   £20.65

MONTGOMERY CHEDDAR

JAMIE MONTGOMERY AND STEVE BRIDGES
MANOR FARM, NORTH CADBURY, SOMERSET

RAW MILK
FRIESIAN COWS
TRAD. ANIMAL   £24.85

Paxton & Whitfield

93 Jermyn Street, London SW1Y 6JE
Tel: 020 7930 0259
Opening times: Mon–Sat 9.30am–6pm, Sun closed
Tube: Piccadilly Circus or Green Park

Jermyn Street is just behind Piccadilly and yet this genteel road, populated by gentlemen's clothing shops and venerable wine and cigar merchants could be a million miles from the city centre. Paxton & Whitfield has the prime spot, backing onto St James's Church and, if you're lucky, you might even hear the bells chime while shopping for your Shropshire Blue. Paxton & Whitfield has been selling its quality cheeses in St James's for 200 years and from its present premises for over 100 years. Having weathered changing tastes and two World Wars during its illustrious history, this shop is living proof that quality produce, knowledge, adaptability and customer service go a long way.

With British farmhouse cheeses now feted all over the world, it's no surprise that they take up half of the massive counter space that runs the length of the shop. Most of the remaining space is dedicated to French cheeses, with a smattering of varieties from other European countries making up the balance. By working directly with British cheese producers, the company can give them vital customer feedback and it also means the staff know every cheese intimately. When it comes to French cheese, Paxton & Whitfield have created a reciprocal partnership with renowned cheesemonger Androuet (page 48), which sources cheeses directly from producers in France. Androuet then rely on the expertise of Paxton & Whitfield for the English cheeses sold in their Parisian shops.

Wander along the groaning counter and you'll find everything from semi-hard goats' cheeses such as Rachel, to sheeps' cheese like Fosseway Fleece. There's Gubbeen from Ireland and the wonderful Fleur du Maquis from Corsica, which is rolled in thyme, chilli and juniper berries. My favourite is the unusual St. Wulfstan, an organic cow's milk cheese with a crumbly texture but wonderfully creamy flavour. The wall opposite the counter contains honey, fruit cheese, confits, mustards and chutneys and there's a room at the back of the shop dedicated to utensils, books, boards, knives and fondue sets. This really is cheese heaven and I dare you to leave empty handed.

While you're in the area...

Fine wine is the perfect partner for fine cheeses and Berry Bros & Rudd (page 158) on nearby St James's Street is a lovely shop packed with history and wine. Head in the other direction, past Piccadilly tube and you'll find all the Japanese food and ingredients you need in the Japan Centre (page 179).

Rippon Cheese Stores

26 Upper Tachbrook Street, London SW1V 1SW
Tel: 020 7931 0628
Opening times: Mon–Fri 8am-5.30pm, Sat 8.30am–5pm
Tube: Victoria or Pimlico

Karen and Philip Rippon have been purveying their enviable collection of fine cheeses to the public from this shop since 1990. During this time, they have steadily built up a reputation for the excellent quality and service they provide and they now supply many restaurants and businesses as well as catering for weddings and corporate functions. When I met Karen she was effusive about all of the 550 varieties of cheese stocked in the purpose-built, temperature-controlled room just inside the shop. The room is crammed full of truckles, portions, sections and wedges of cheese from all over Europe and the smell is intoxicating. There are endless blues and goats' cheeses, there's Vacherin and Morbier and there's a really good selection of English farmhouse cheese such as the semi-soft Lord London, the hard ewes' milk cheese, Lord of the Hundreds, and the tangy Sussex Farmhouse.

For the novice, there's no particular order to the cheeses in the room but Karen knows exactly where everything is and the neat displays demonstrate the care and attention that is given to the selection and storage of the cheese. A small area at the front of the shop doubles up as a tiny grocery store, offering partners for your cheese purchases, such as biscuits, preserves and chutneys, plus a few sweet treats like macaroons and madeleines.

While you're in the area...

The wacky sweet shop, Chocodeli is next door and is a great place to complement your savoury purchases with sweet ones. If you want some freshly baked bread to go with your cheese, take a short stroll to the lovely French bakery, Poilâne (page 26) on Elizabeth Street.

RIPPON CHEESE STORE
A ONE OFF
1 DAY CLOSURE

SATURDAY 25TH JUNE

CHEE
FERS

mment
LUCERNI
wiss £12/
a land hard

CHOCOLATIERS

Young or old, male or female, most people have a weakness for chocolate, and London has a host of fabulous chocolatiers where even the sweetest tooth can be indulged. For a real treat why not head to Angel and visit Paul A. Young (see page 68) for a true taste of heaven. Or if you find youself in Knightsbridge stop off at Rococo Chocolates (see page 69) where you can take a class in chocolate making at their renowned Chocolate School. Theobroma Cacao (see page 71) in Turnham Green has a great rage of chocolates for kids to keep the little people in your life happy. Go on, indulge!

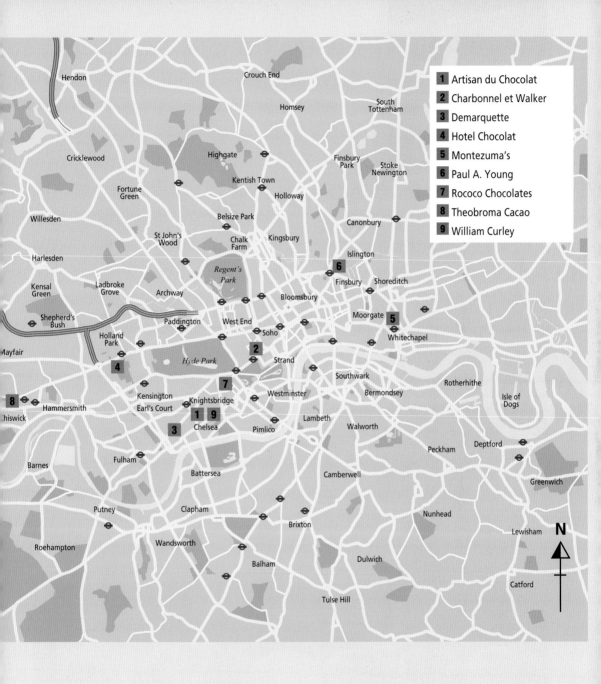

1 Artisan du Chocolat
2 Charbonnel et Walker
3 Demarquette
4 Hotel Chocolat
5 Montezuma's
6 Paul A. Young
7 Rococo Chocolates
8 Theobroma Cacao
9 William Curley

Artisan du Chocolat

89 Lower Sloane Street, London SW1W 8DA
Tel: 0845 2706996
Opening times: Mon–Sat 10am–7pm, Sun 12pm–5pm
Tube: Sloane Square or Knightsbridge

This renowned London chocolatier is close enough to the King's Road to be easily accessible from all over town but still sufficiently tucked away to make you feel like you've made a real discovery when you step inside. Indeed, a visit to Artisan is a bit like winning one of Willy Wonka's elusive golden tickets: it's a magical world of incredibly clever and exciting chocolate creations that taste every bit as good as they look. The dark wooden counters echo the richness of the cocoa that is displayed in endless incarnations around the shop. Truffles reign supreme in one long counter, with the selection of best-selling liquid salted caramels taking pride of place. These delicate little spheres literally burst open in your mouth to reveal gorgeous liquid caramel and it's easy to see why they've taken the chocolate world by storm. The packaging is wonderfully creative, with all the salted caramel boxes emulating expensive face creams. South Sea pearls are silver and gold-coated ganaches that look like jewels rather than edibles, and the Chapel Down Truffle does indeed have the subtle flavour of the English sparkling wine that gives it its name. Couture chocolates are available to buy singly or in beautiful presentation boxes, whilst bars come in a number of country-specific cocoas (my favourite is Haiti 72%), or infused flavours such as Ginger & Lemongrass, Espresso, and Tobacco.

All the chocolates are made at the company's workshop in Ashford and Artisan is fairly unusual amongst chocolatiers, in that it does the conching and refining of its beans on site. This means it has complete control over the flavour, texture, and quality of the final product and it shows.

Other London branches:

81 Westbourne Grove, London W2 4UL
Selfridges, 400 Oxford Street, London W1

While you're in the area...

Take a walk along King's Road and stop off at Partridges (page 153) in Duke of York Square: it's a one-stop grocery and deli. Head the other direction onto Pimlico Road and you'll reach the equally lovely Daylesford Organic (page 148), with its cool interior and buzzing café.

Charbonnel et Walker

One The Royal Arcade, 28 Old Bond Street,
London W1S 4BT
Tel: 020 7491 0939
Opening times: Mon-Sat 10am–6pm, Sun closed
Tube: Green Park

As one of the oldest chocolatiers in London, Charbonnel et Walker has a deserved place in the city's food heritage. The company was founded back in 1875 and was the result of the collaboration between Mrs Walker and Madame Charbonnel, who came to England from a prestigious Parisian chocolatier. Although the address has changed, there has always been a shop on Bond Street and the current location is like a chocolate box itself, with its gorgeous rounded bay window and eccentrically disproportionate interior dimensions. The shop is long and narrow with various displays of its unctuous wares giving off delightful aromas and encouraging you to immerse yourself in chocolate decadence.

Classic individual chocolates are lined up beneath the main counter but if you can't narrow down your choice, you can always just go for one of the box selections with their distinctive, classy packaging. The truffles here are legendary and there are boxes of these as well, including Champagne, vanilla, and strawberry varieties, all handmade at the company's production unit in Tunbridge Wells. There is also a range of chocolate bars and my personal favourite is the Dark Chocolate Ginger, which I always buy if I'm passing by. But, if I run out of drinking chocolate, I'll make a detour: this is the best I've ever tasted with its large flakes of chocolate and rich, creamy flavour.

Other London branches:

Cabot Place West, Canary Wharf, London E14 4QT
Liverpool Street Station, London EC2M 7PY

While you're in the area...

Fortnum & Mason (page 107) is very close by on Piccadilly and you really shouldn't head home without visiting one of the best food halls in the capital. If you walk in the other direction, around Berkeley Square, you can pay a visit to Allen's of Mayfair (page 30) for some quality meat.

Demarquette

285 Fulham Road, London SW10 9PZ
Tel: 020 7351 5467
Opening times: Tues–Thurs 11am–6pm, Fri–Sat
11am–7pm, Sun–Mon closed
Tube: South Kensington

Marc Demarquette made a life-changing decision while he was lying in a hospital bed after a serious accident. He decided to give up his career to follow his heart and his passion for chocolate. Although born and raised in London, his French ancestry meant he had spent many childhood holidays in France and it was here that he returned with one mission in mind: to learn how to create exquisite hand-made chocolates in the traditional French style. He spent years honing his skills with Master Chocolatiers before he felt ready to open his own chocolate boutique in London. He now has a loyal clientele, a wall covered with awards and he is also the House Chocolatier for Fortnum & Mason.

Marc describes his work as 'directing an orchestra of flavours' and once you've tried his chocolate, you'll know exactly what he's talking about. The cocoa flavour is at the heart of everything in the shop and additional flavours work in harmony with it, rather than overpowering it. Marc works with the highest quality ethically sourced chocolate and single origin beans, which even extends to the couveture (coating) for the ganaches. It might seem like a small detail but try a Pure Cocoa Single Origin ganache and you'll appreciate it. The intensity of the cocoa flavour makes your palate tingle but it's remarkably smooth at the same time. The Salted Caramel Heart with its Cornish sea salt and Cornish milk is wonderfully subtle and this celebration of British ingredients can also be seen in his unique seasonal collections, which have included English Garden, Great British Orchard, and Alice in Wonderland. However, for me, the Moroccan Mint Tea ganache perfectly sums up Marc's talent: it doesn't just taste of mint, or mint tea, it tastes exactly like Moroccan mint tea. If you've ever sipped tea in the Djemaa el Fna square in Marrakech, you'll be instantly transported back there with this ganache – truly incredible.

While you're in the area...

If you walk north along Fulham Road you'll come across a number of gourmet treats. Lea & Sandeman (page 162) wine merchants is a minute further on the other side of the road. If you stay on the same side, it's just a couple of minutes' walk to Luigi's (page 82), a typical Italian deli with daily specials to take away.

Hotel Chocolat

163 Kensington High Street, London W8 6SU
Tel: 020 7938 2144
Opening times: Mon–Fri 9.30am–7.30pm, Sat
9.30am–7pm, Sun 11am–6pm
Tube: High Street Kensington

This long, spacious shop is too inviting to walk past and the addition of the small café and cosy leather sofas make it almost impossible to resist the temptations of a hot chocolate or coffee, which come with a couple of chocolates on the side. The cocoa-coloured interior makes for luxurious browsing and the shelves are neatly arranged to showcase the different ranges of chocolate made by the company.

The Hotel Chocolat range encompasses everything from fun nibbles and chocolate lollies to bars for self-indulgence and the serious Signature Collection for connoisseurs and gift givers. The company has its own cocoa plantation in Saint Lucia and the Rabot Estate provides the raw material for many of the products you see in the shop. This gives the customer the benefit of knowing the entire story behind their bar or box of chocolates and the company complete creative control from bean to bar. The Purist range of bars is the ideal way to sample and compare the subtle differences between single origin chocolates.

Other London branches

Rabot Estate, 2 Stoney Street, London SE1 9AA
New Fetter Lane, London EC4A 3BN
43 Cheapside, One New Change, London EC2V 6AH
5 Montpelier Street, London SW7 1EZ
16 Leadenhall Market, City of London, EC3V 1LR
The Vaults, Lower Concourse, London Bridge Station,
London SE1 9SP
Moorgate Hall, 143-171 Moorgate, London EC2M 6XB
78 The Strand, London WC2R 0DE
133 Victoria Street, London SW1E 6RD

While you're in the area...

The cavernous Whole Foods Market (page 120) is just down the road and is an organic shop of supermarket proportions. Take a side turn down Argyll Street and try one of the fresh pizza slices or artisan loaves from Exeter Street Bakery (page 20).

Montezuma's

51 Brushfield Street, London E1 6AA
Tel: 020 7539 9208
Opening times: Mon 11am–4pm, Tues–Sun 10am–6pm
Tube: Liverpool Street or Shoreditch High Street

The best ideas can come about as a result of monumental life changes and Montezuma's is no exception. Founders, Helen and Simon Pattinson, gave up their lucrative City law careers to go travelling around South America. A stay on a cocoa plantation planted the seed of a new venture and the chocolate-obsessed couple set up their first shop in Brighton just a year after returning from their travels. There are now five shops, including the gorgeous store in Spitalfields, all selling the distinctive chocolate that has seen Montezuma's take one of the top spots in the London cocoa world.

The shop is spotless, the shelves are full and the staff are poised to help but the chocolate itself is infused with such a sense of fun and creativity that you just walk around smiling. It's like a grown-up sweet shop with bars, jars, blocks and boxes of chocolates and truffles. Personally, I like to have a stash of Butterscotch, and Orange & Geranium bars at home but there's a huge range to choose from including Chilli & Lime, Coconut, Nutmeg, as well as regular milk, dark and creamy white.

With a name that derives from the Aztec Emperor, Montecuhzoma, it's no surprise that much of the organic cocoa used to make this fine collection of treats comes from a co-op in Peru, with the rest being sourced from the Dominican Republic. The ethos at Montezuma's has always been to pay a fair price to farmers but the deal works both ways: this is seriously good stuff.

While you're in the area...

One of the best cheesemongers in London, Androuet (page 48), is a close neighbour. Leave the market and cross over Brushfield Street to discover the two tiny foodie delights of A. Gold (page 144) and Verde & Co. Both are well worth visiting. If you're here on Sunday, you can check out Spitalfields Market and Brick Lane Upmarket (page 129).

Paul A. Young

33 Camden Passage, London N1 8EA
Tel: 020 7424 5750
Opening times: Mon closed, Tues–Thurs
10am–6.30pm, Fri 10am–7pm, Sat 10am–6.30pm,
Sun 11am–5pm
Tube: Angel

If you ever need a quick hit of chocolate indulgence, step inside Paul A. Young and buy a Rum & Raisin truffle. You'll immediately be transported far from this mortal coil to a place of immense pleasure. In fact, you can buy any of the truffles here and experience the same effect: this just happens to be my favourite. Each chocolate is lovingly handmade on the premises every day and brought upstairs to the cosy shop, which oozes cocoa extravagance from every pore. From the plum-coloured shop front to the wooden floors, the immaculate displays and the dizzy aroma of fresh chocolate, this is a little den of decadence tucked away in a charming side street in Angel.

If you like your chocolate in bar form, there's plenty of choice: purists have a range of dark Venezuelan, Madagascan and Dominican bars, or you can go leftfield with Green Pepper, Edible Gold Leaf, or Paul's award-winning Sea-Salted Caramel Bar. But it's the truffles that will really take your breath away. The counter is like an artist's palette and, when I was

there, I was lucky to see the artist himself, busy working on a batch of new chocolates. Paul works with classic flavours but there are some surprises too with truffles such as Marmite, and Port and Stilton showing off his creativity and proving the versatility of the main ingredient. Treat yourself, or someone else, to anything from this shop and you'll never touch mass-produced sweets again.

Other London branches
20 Royal Exchange, Threadneedle Street, London EC3V 3LP

While you're in the area...
Angel is a heavenly food destination and you can't walk more than a few steps along Upper Street without encountering a gem of a shop, café or bakery. Take the weight off your feet in Euphorium (page 19) and sample some of their fabulous sandwiches and pastries, then try a tipple or two at The Sampler (page 167). Finally, head up to Penton Street and stock up on Italian treats in Olga Stores (page 83).

Rococo Chocolates

5 Motcomb Street, London SW1X 8JU
Tel: 020 7245 0993
Opening hours: Mon 12pm–5pm, Tues–Sat
10am–6.30pm, Sun 12pm–5pm
Tube: Knightsbridge

This is the flagship store and stepping inside is like walking into the prettiest front room you've ever been in. There are sofas, colourful cabinets and farmhouse tables and chairs. But, whilst there's plenty of room to sit and relax with a hot drink and a chocolate treat, most of the space is filled with beautiful bars, bags and boxes of edible goodies. At the back of the shop, a window overlooks a tiny courtyard garden, which opens to customers in the summer. There's also a glass panel in the shop floor allowing a peek into the downstairs kitchen and Chocolate School, where you can learn everything from tempering to truffle making.

The saying 'like a child in a sweet shop' could have been coined for this shop, as you really can't take it all in with just one circuit of the spacious room: there's too much to absorb. Whilst the chocolate produced in the central West Norwood kitchen is of the highest quality, Rococo has managed to combine this with a good dollop of fun and you'll come across everything from chocolate asparagus and hand-painted dark chocolate crocodiles, to real hen eggs filled with praline. It's therefore no great surprise to discover that founder, Chantal Coady, comes from a design background: the shop and its contents are bursting with creativity and ingenuity.

The truffle flavours are no less intriguing and include Cherry in Cognac, Rum and Lychee, and Jasmine Tea and the big counter display allows you to pick and choose your favourites to fill varying sized boxes. When it comes to the organic and artisan bars – of which there are 50 different varieties –

much of the cocoa used to make them comes from the company's own plantation in Granada, which involves the farmers in every step of the process and ensures a good price for their crops.

Other London branches:

45 Marylebone High Street, London W1U 5HG

321 Kings Road, London SW3 5EP

While you're in the area...

Hop across the road to Ottolenghi deli (page 84) for some delectable pastries and savoury goodies. You're also just minutes away from two of the best food halls in the capital. Harrods (page 109) and Harvey Nichols (page 111) have superlative gourmet emporiums and you should set aside some serious shopping time for both.

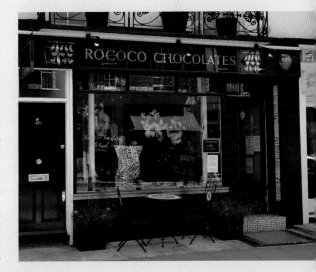

Theobroma Cacao

43 Turnham Green Terrace, London W4 1RG
Tel: 020 8996 0431
Opening times: Mon–Sat 9am–6pm, Sun closed
Tube: Turnham Green

Many people regard this as one of the best chocolatiers in London and, having perused the shelves and tasted some of the offerings prepared in the downstairs kitchen, I'd have to agree. It's hard to believe that such a varied and delectable selection of cacao goodies could be produced in this beautiful little shop but every square inch of the interior has been given over to the bean. Co-founder Phil Neal made the natural leap from patissier to chocolatier in 1999 and people now travel from all over town to sample his creations. Phil works with natural ingredients and high-quality cocoa beans to create some of the best chocolate you'll ever pop in your mouth.

There's a huge range of truffles including Champagne, Grand Marnier and Violet, Almond and Pistachio, then there's fruit-dipped chocolate, chocolate figurines, and a selection of bars – I'd recommend the Sea Salt Dark Chocolate, which I greedily devoured in one sitting. There's also a range of kids' chocolates and bars and a stunning selection of gift boxes, where even the boxes themselves are handmade. Phil and his team also make their own ice cream and sorbet and a fantastic range of seasonal treats throughout the year. And, if you like your chocolate in liquid form, there's a small hot chocolate bar in the shop where you can try out anything from the 'house' vanilla hot chocolate, to something more unusual like banana, chilli or cinnamon.

While you're in the area...

Cross the road for a wonderful selection of free range and organic meat at Macken Brothers Ltd. If you stay on the same side of the road you're practically next door to the lovely Mortimer & Bennett deli and the highly regarded Covent Garden Fishmonger (page 95).

William Curley

198 Ebury Street, London SW1W 8UN
Tel: 020 7730 5522
Opening times: Mon–Thurs 9am–7pm,
Fri–Sat 9am–8pm, Sun 10am–6pm
Tube: Sloane Square

Serious chocoholics flock to this pretty little shop to indulge their sweet tooth with some of the best patisserie and chocolate in town. The shop is welcoming and customers are encouraged to take the weight off their feet at one of the tables in order to give their undivided attention to some of the vast range of outstanding creations on offer here. William and his wife, Suzue, have both enjoyed illustrious careers in the world of food – patisserie in particular – so their two shops are a natural evolution and the perfect way in which they can indulge their creativity and demonstrate their rare skills.

Everything you see is handmade in the kitchen here, or in the sister shop in Richmond, and the counters are full of exquisite pastries, truffles and ganaches that really push the boundaries of couture chocolate making. Chocolate flavours range from the eminently popular Sea Salt Caramel and Richmond Park Honey, to more unusual creations like Apricot and Wasabi, and my personal favourite, the moreish Orange and Balsamic Vinegar. William works exclusively with a small Tuscan chocolate supplier called Amedei, and this ensures the consistency of quality that he has become famous for.

The shop has a wonderfully laid-back feel for a high-end chocolatier. You can sit down and enjoy hot drinks, pancakes, pastries and homemade ice cream in flavours like basil and green tea during the week, and from Friday to Sunday the kitchen also offers a quirky but stunning Dessert Bar Menu. This is surely the ultimate way to give in to your sugar cravings; it's like a miniature four-course meal comprised solely of desserts. The menu changes regularly so it's the perfect excuse to skip lunch and come straight here for the dessert menu. If you're suitably impressed, you can book a place on one of the many courses that William and his team offer in the downstairs kitchen and learn some of the secrets of chocolate for yourself.

Other London branches:
10 Paved Court, Richmond, Surrey TW9 1LZ

While you're in the area...
You're just a few short paces away from the stunning Daylesford Organic shop and café (page 148), where you can browse the shelves and stop for a bite to eat. Another couple of minutes' easy walking towards Victoria will bring you to the French bakery Poilâne (page 26) where fresh baked is baked 24 hours a day.

MARZIPAN
Tender marzipan coated in
Toscano 66% chocolate
ORANGE
PISTACHIO
TOASTED
£2.50 each

DELICATESSENS

London is blessed with a whole variety of wonderful delicatessens. Indeed, in some parts of the capital it seems as if you can't turn a street corner without hapenning upon another inviting-looking establishment, beconing you inside with its tempting window display! In this section you will find the pick of the bunch, from the truly fantastic Ottolenghi (see page 84) and the kosher specialist Panzer's (see page 87) in the North, to the quaint Trinity Stores (see poage 89) and the East Dulwich Deli (see page 78), with its own bakery, in the South.

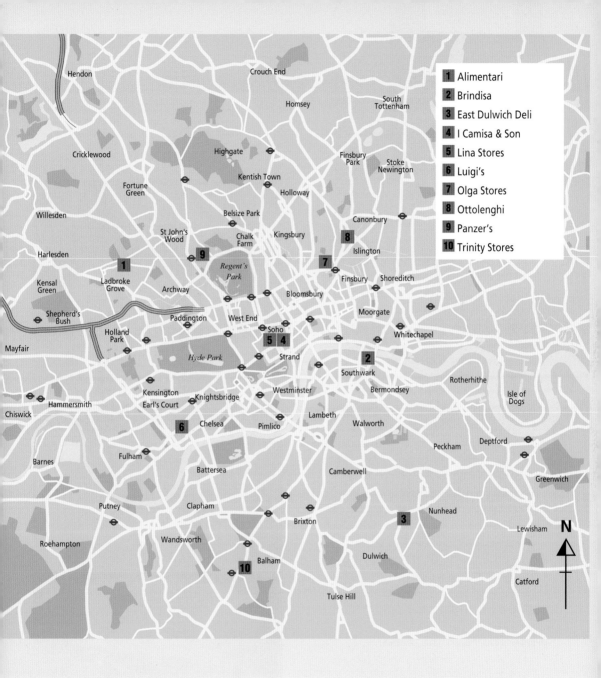

1 Alimentari
2 Brindisa
3 East Dulwich Deli
4 I Camisa & Son
5 Lina Stores
6 Luigi's
7 Olga Stores
8 Ottolenghi
9 Panzer's
10 Trinity Stores

Alimentari

342 Kilburn Lane, London W9 3EF
Tel: 020 8969 3999
Opening times: Mon–Thurs 9am–7.30pm, Fri 9am–10pm, Sat–Sun 10am–6pm
Tube: Queen's Park

This Queen's Park deli is a haven for locals in need of a quality cappuccino and a little something to have on the side. It's neither quaint nor quirky but strikes a balance firmly down the middle with uber contemporary fixtures and fittings sitting happily alongside distressed tables and dressers. Every last packet of pasta is displayed to its maximum vantage and the food is treated with that Italian reverence that we've learnt to appreciate. You'll find everything here from biscotti to Bresaola and it's a truly delightful shop to explore with little nooks and crannies, shelves, baskets and boxes all neatly stacked and laden down with Italian goodies. There's Umbrian preserves, Sicilian sea salt, homemade fresh pasta and sauces, specialist dried pastas, balsamic vinegar, olive oil, olives and pâté. There are cheeses, hams and fresh bread and a gorgeous selection of cakes and pastries.

However, the business doesn't stop with the deli. Alimentari also runs a successful catering service, with a range of homemade food to order. Staff also create bespoke food hampers and run weekly Friday night wine tastings, as well as other one-off food events. This is far more than a local shop; Alimentari is an all-encompassing food emporium on a glorious gourmand mission.

While you're in the area...

If you walk north for about 10–15 minutes you'll discover The Olive Tree, a lovely little grocery and health food shop with a couple of tables so you can sit and linger.

Brindisa

Stoney Street, Borough Market, London SE1 9AF
Tel: 020 7407 1036
Opening times: Tues–Thurs 10am–5.30pm, Fri
10am–6pm, Sat 8.30am–5pm
Tube: London Bridge or Borough

This spacious Spanish deli calls Borough Market its home but despite one doorway leading out into the heart of the marketplace, Brindisa manages to provide some much-needed breathing space from the rush hour trading traffic of Borough on market days. The shelves are beautifully arranged with Spanish specialities and there's plenty of choice in every category. Olive oil is available in industrial cans down to small bottles and the sherry vinegar is treated like vintage wine with its gorgeous packaging and spacious arrangement. Separate counters for specific products make browsing easy and it's possible to tick items off your shopping list as you move from one counter to the next.

There are artisan cheeses, salt cod, olive pâté, anchovies, smoked Marcona almonds, quince paste, and a whole section dedicated to beans, peas and lentils. As you'd expect in a quality Spanish deli, the range of charcouterie is breathtaking. You'll find black pudding, fresh and cured chorizo, as well as Iberico and Serrano ham, which is hand-carved to order. In fact, the art of carving Spanish ham is so highly regarded that the shop now runs courses in which you can learn knife skills from the experts and taste a range of hams. When you've finished shopping you can step outside to the grill and try a sizzling Brindisa chorizo roll. Which is exactly what I did and I'd highly recommend them.

While you're in the area...

Borough Market is crammed with some of the best food producers and independent food shops in the capital so try and see as much as you can while you're there. Arrive early as the whole place is heaving by 10am. When it's time for a coffee break head to Monmouth Coffee and when it's time for lunch, join the justifiable queue for Tapas Brindisa, or grab a quick bite at one of the many food stalls in the market.

East Dulwich Deli

15–17 Lordship Lane, London SE22 8EW

Tel: 020 8693 2525

Opening Times: Mon–Sat 9am–6pm, Sun 10am–4pm

Train: East Dulwich

When owners Tony and Tracey were looking for a bread supplier for their new deli, they couldn't find the quality they wanted. However, instead of settling for second best, they set up their own bakery, 'Born and Bread'. It's a traditional bakery where handcrafted sourdough loaves are baked in a wood-fired oven. It now supplies over 80 clients, including their own shop, and it's this meticulous attention to quality and detail that has attracted a loyal following for this local deli that opened ten years ago.

The staff are incredibly passionate about food and there's not much they don't know about the hundreds of products that are stocked in this vast gourmand gallery. A fresh deli counter stretches the full depth of the shop and is stocked with cheeses, charcouterie, salads, cakes and savouries, ready to take away. The bread counter groans under the weight of freshly baked loaves and the smell is enough to make your wallet jump out of your pocket of its own accord. I went for the five-flour, five-seed sourdough and it tormented me all the way home. Luckily, I had an Olive Grissini to keep me going. Baked exclusively for East Dulwich Deli and Harrods, this salty, chewy snack is absolutely sublime.

Moving through to the second room of the Deli, you'll discover a floor-to-ceiling display of beautifully packaged pasta, antipasti and sauces, as well as olive oil, chutneys, preserves, crackers, biscuits and pickles. The whole shop is light, spacious, packed with all manner of goodies and ideally suited to browsing. What more could you ask for?

While you're in the area...

Lordship Lane has pretty much everything you could possibly want and need in a shopping street. Moxon's fishmonger (page 100) and William Rose butcher (page 45) are at the other end of the street but you should make a stop at Cheeseblock (page 49) on the way. Green Cuisine is a lovely kitchen shop and Dulwich Supermarket offers a great selection of Turkish, Greek and Mediterranean produce and ingredients.

Montgomery's Cheddar.

Traditional cloth bound cheese from Somerset. Fully matured and a fruity spicy flavour

Bree De Melun

From Nothern France. Rich, creamy and moist.

Monte Enebro

Rich, earth goats cheese from Spain.

Mahortoga

Mature Spanish ewes milk cheese.

Swaledale

Light, fresh, nutty goats cheese from North Yorkshire

Taleggio

Soft, mild creamy cheese from Italy.

Born and Bread
Organic Bakery

Hand crafted bread made with stoneground flour and natural starters, and baked in a woodfired oven.

Small white loaf £1·85   Wholemeal £1·90
Large white loaf £3·25
100% Rye Sourdough £3·35   Large Wholemeal £3·30
                            Kentish Flute £1·45

"A Joy to eat" - Nigel Slater - The Observer

i Camisa & Son

61 Old Compton Street, London W1D 6HS
Tel: 020 7437 7610
Opening times: Mon–Sat 8.30am–6pm, Sun closed
Tube: Leicester Square or Piccadilly Circus

The Soho area has always been a magnet for the Italian community so it's only natural that the number of quality delis in this area is disproportionately high. I Camisa & Son is just around the corner from Lina Stores but it offers an entirely different shopping experience. The busy window display is packed with fresh loaves, huge chunks of cheese and Italian cakes whilst inside, the small shop is dominated by a vast glass counter. You'll be spotted by a member of staff long before you've had a chance to take everything in, let alone chosen what to order but that's mere efficiency on their part and there's no pressure to make a hasty decision. Old grocery cabinets house a selection of rice, pulses, pasta and grains, as well as other must-have Italian ingredients. However, it's the fresh, homemade pasta that i Camisa is known for and it's lined up in the counter, along with salads, marinated olives, grilled vegetables and various antipasti. I saw a number of filled ravioli when I visited, as well as tortellini and handmade tagliatelle.

Aside from the pasta, there's a selection of cheese in the deli section, and a long list of charcouterie such as Mortadella, Toscano Milano, Pancetta and Chorizo, which are all sliced to order. Bottles of olive oil top the already giddying heights of the serving counter and the sawdust on the floor seems to be there to remind customers that this is one of the great, authentic London Italian delis – as if you could forget.

While you're in the area...

Pop around the corner to Brewer Street to the fabulous, refurbished Lina Stores (opposite) or head to Chinatown for a spot of lunch, followed by ingredients shopping in Loon Fung (page 181).

Lina Stores

18 Brewer Street, London W1F 0SH
Tel: 020 7437 6482
Opening times: Mon–Fri 9am–6.30pm, Sat
9am–5.30pm, Sun closed
Tube: Piccadilly Circus

When Gabriella's parents bought Lina Stores in 1978, it had already been a deli since 1944. In fact, you can still see some of the original boxes that Lina used to transport her precious cargo of olive oil and other Italian delicacies from her native Genoa. Lina sounds like a feisty character but I'm sure she would have approved of the current owners' continued dedication in their quest to bring an authentic slice of Italy to the centre of Soho.

The shop was completely refurbished in November 2010 in order to open up the space and allow customers a more hands-on shopping experience. Vast floor-to-ceiling shelves offer a gastronomic tour of Italy from rice, pasta and antipasti through to biscuits, sweets, honey and olive oil. The other side of the shop is dedicated to classic deli produce and there's a huge range of quality cured and dried meats like Coppa, Speak, Pancetta and Salame Milano. The cheese selection is no less impressive with Fontina, Pecorino, Toma and Tellagio lined up inside the glass counter. Sacks of loose beans and lentils are ready to be weighed out and there's a small selection of fruit and vegetables, plus a counter full of fresh loaves supplied by Tichini and Exeter Street bakeries.

When I visited, Gabriella's husband was busy creating his signature handmade pasta in the downstairs kitchen and this is also where the couple make fresh pasta sauces and sausages. For me, this is what makes a deli stand out from the crowd: freshly made food combined with the best ingredients; food that you just can't buy anywhere else. And, with its green cotton candy awning and colour scheme, Lina Stores is also as pretty as a picture.

While you're in the area...

If one deli just isn't enough on a gourmet day out then walk around the corner to Old Compton Street and step inside i Camisa & Son (opposite) for even more delectable fresh and dried pasta.

Luigi's

349 Fulham Road, London SW10 9TW
Tel: 020 7352 7739
Opening times: Mon–Fri 9am–9.30pm,
Sat 9am–7pm, Sun closed
Tube: Fulham Broadway or South Kensington

The best Italian delis in London have survived foodie fads, recessions, local demolition and regeneration programmes, trendy rival openings and the onslaught of the mega supermarkets. Luigi's is one such example of the endurance of well-sourced, quality ingredients and it has been proudly serving its fiercely loyal clientele since 1973. This fact in itself should be enough for you to make your way over to

the Fulham Road and check it out but longevity is far from the only jewel in its crown. Step inside this classically laid out deli and you're transported to Italy. Staff bustle around in smart red uniforms, working in that unique, chaotic Italian way that gets things done with just the right combination of activity, gesticulation and animated banter. If you want a lesson in multi-tasking, this is a great place to see it in action. It was a busy lunchtime when I visited and meat was being sliced while food orders were being taken and regulars were engaged in conversation by the staff.

The range of food here is superlative and it begins with a window packed with produce, bread and groceries. There are beautiful crates of fresh fruit, and a large charcouterie counter with everything from Spinata Romana and Bresaola, to charcoal roasted ham. There's fresh homemade pasta to take away, a huge range of dried pastas and sauces, estate bottled olive oils and a good choice of farmhouse cheese. But the real draw in Luigi's is the incredible range of fresh meals that are prepared in the little kitchen at the back of the shop. As well as salads, pasta, pesto and vegetable dishes, the chefs come up with daily specials like Saltimbocca, and Cannelloni, ensuring local workers never have to buy a production line sandwich for lunch.

While you're in the area...

If there's any space left in your shopping bag fill it with some chocolate treats from Demarquette (page 65) then stop off at Lea & Sandeman (page 162) for a well-chosen bottle of wine to go with your food.

Olga Stores

30 Penton Street, London N1 9PS
Tel: 020 7837 5467
Opening times: Mon–Sat 8am–8pm,
Sun 10am–4pm
Tube: Angel

I used to live just across the road from Olga Stores so I have a soft spot for this delightfully unpretentious and authentic Italian deli. I've got so many fond memories of popping in after work for some fresh pasta and sauce and a nice bottle of wine. When I went back, the shop was much as I remembered: shelves bursting with a huge range of Italian goodies and baskets of fresh fruit and vegetables using up the already diminutive floor space. Although the range of fresh pasta is now much depleted, the homemade lasagne is still a crowd-pleaser and people travel here specially to take home one of these rich, meaty meals. A steady stream of lunchtime customers also pops in for one of the freshly prepared sandwiches, with smoked salmon and Mortadella being particularly prized.

Seasonal treats such as black truffles are another draw and there's a well-stocked cheese counter with Pecorino, Tellagio and Manchego vying for space. It goes without saying that the range of dried pasta, rice, antipasti, sauces and dried mushrooms is superlative, and big bowls of olives and freshly made baccala croquettes are perfect for snacking. The delicate custard tarts with their distinctive sweet, eggy filling are too tempting to ignore and you'll be glad you didn't – they're delicious.

While you're in the area...

Keep walking south along Penton Street and you'll get to Amwell Street. Here you'll find Unpackaged, a beautiful grocery shop where you bring up and fill up your own containers with organic wholefoods, tea, coffee, spices, dried fruit, nuts and seeds. Walk north and you'll reach Chapel Market in a matter of seconds, with its varied stalls and market banter. Another minute will bring you onto Upper Street where Euphorium (page 19), The Sampler (page 167) and Ottolenghi (page 84) await.

Ottolenghi

287 Upper Street, London N1 2TZ
Tel: 020 7288 1454
Opening times: Mon–Sat 8am–11pm,
Sun 9am–7pm
Tube: Angel or Highbury & Islington

Yotam Ottolenghi has carved out a new niche in the food market with his gorgeous, upmarket delicatessens serving food that you'd love to be able to prepare yourself, if only you had the time and the necessary skill and imagination. The Islington branch is the largest of the four delis and the only one to include a sit-down restaurant that opens for breakfast then keeps serving all day, right through to dinner in the evening when reservations are essential to secure one of the much sought-after tables.

The super sleek interior with its minimalist white styling and distinctive flashes of signature red allows the food displays to sing. The front of the shop is dedicated to take-away food then the long, slender space beyond merges seamlessly into the 50-cover café. The glorious salad bar puts its

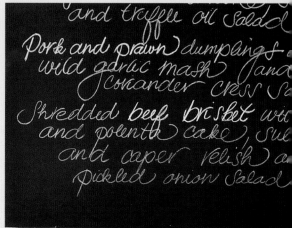

Cured mackerel with pickled
vegetables broad bean and
confit garlic yoghurt

Ricotta and basil stuffed
courgette   with
         wild   ey,
pine nut
lemon

sweetcorn

Take away

- small salad box
- large salad box
- mains sold separately

Cheese Straw

Granola Bar

Cheese and Chard pie

competitors to shame and dishes such as basmati with peas, green beans with pomegranate, and seared tuna slices make it difficult to make a decision for a take away lunch. A huge basket of freshly baked bread, as well as shelves of cereals, nuts, seeds, jams and other groceries add to the shopping decisions and then there's the cake section, which is virtually impossible to ignore. Chocolate cups, hazelnut brownies, little lemon mascarpone tarts and individual plum crumbles are just some of the sweet treats on offer in this beautifully appointed shop and café that hits the upmarket food nail firmly on the head.

Other London branches:

63 Ledbury Road, London W11 2AD

1 Holland Street, London W8 4NA

13 Motcomb Street, London SW1X 8LB

While you're in the area...

Buy your fresh fish and seafood from Steve Hatt (page 103), which is just around the corner on Essex Road. Paul A. Young (page 68) creates amazing chocolates in his shop in Camden Passage, and Euphorium bakery (page 19) is just up the road towards Highbury & Islington tube.

Panzer's

13-19 Circus Road, London NW8 6PB
Tel: 020 7586 2067
Opening times: Mon–Fri 8am–7pm,
Sat 8am–6pm, Sun 8am–2pm
Tube: St John's Wood

Panzer's has been delighting the residents of St John's Wood with its incredible range of deli products, kosher food and American favourites for over 50 years. It remains a family-run business and enjoys catering to the diverse clientele that passes through its doors each day. The range and variety of products has evolved over the years to reflect the changing nature of the area but its Jewish roots remain at the heart of the business. The entire exterior of the large shop is lined with thoughtfully displayed fruit and vegetables including white asparagus, Barhi grapes and Sharon fruit. Inside, Panzer's is like a plush combination of grocery store and deli and, indeed, it's the massive deli counter that has the wow factor. Here, pickled herring, smoked salmon and mackerel, paprika salami, liver sausage and numerous cheeses, salads, dips and olives are all displayed with pride, but there's also a good selection of packaged fish, frozen meat and ready meals.

Moving on around the shop you'll find dried fruit and nuts, groceries and classics from across the pond such as Saltines, Mircale Whip, Hershey bars and Graham Crackers. Speciality breads are brought in from bakeries such as Rinkoff, Exeter Street and The Flour Station and there's everything from tortano to Irish soda bread and walnut levain. Oh, and of course, bagels. You could spend hours just browsing the shelves here, there's so much to explore and whether you're looking for a nostalgic taste of home, or you're trying out new ingredients, it's one to bookmark.

While you're in the area...

The glorious Gail's bakery (page 22) is also on Circus Road and is deserved of some time out from your schedule. For exceptional seafood you only have to walk two minutes away to Brown's (page 92). If you want to stretch your legs, Yeoman's greengrocer (page 154) is a pleasant half hour stroll away on Regent's Park Road.

Trinity Stores

5&6 Balham Station Road, London SW12 9SG
Tel: 020 8673 3773
Opening times: Mon–Fri 9am–8pm, Sat 9.30am–5.30pm, Sun 10am–5pm
Tube: Balham

Walking into Trinity Stores is like stepping inside a quaint farm shop in the countryside. It is warm and cosy, calm and comforting and you'll be wrapped up in its blanket of good food, endearing service and community spirit within seconds. Although the road itself is hardly a shopping destination, the shop's proximity to the station and the High Street both act in its favour, though I got the impression that regulars travelled here from much further afield to avail of the fantastic range of products and the genial atmosphere.

Graeme Fisher and George Hornby opened Trinity Stores in 2007 and their design choices of mismatched tables and chairs, notice boards full of local events, and appetising, homemade food is pitch perfect. The fresh food counter is full of the kind of food you'd like to make for lunch if time and store cupboards allowed. Scotch eggs, tarts, gorgeous salads, homemade cakes and cookies are all made locally in keeping with the ethos of the deli: to use small, regional independent producers and suppliers and those with a genuine commitment to their food. Much of the food is sourced from the British Isles and seasonality is important. The cheese counter is stocked with a generous selection of Neal's Yard Dairy cheeses, including Berkswell, Wigmore and Spenwood. Then there's organic fruit and vegetables from Kent, regional British beer and yogurt, butter and ice cream from Cornwall. The grocery section is stocked with a select range of both British and Italian goodies, including Stokes sauces and delicious regional olive oils.

The little café area plays host to regular wine tasting evenings where producers come and talk about their wine, and delicious homemade food helps to soak up the alcohol. With an outside catering arm to the business as well, this quality deli is a real all-rounder.

While you're in the area...

If you wander around the corner onto Balham High Road, you'll find the health food gem, As Nature Intended, which is like a little supermarket dedicated to the good things in life.

FISHMONGERS

Be it fish and chips that takes your fancy, a Spanish-themed seafood paella or perhaps you're splashing out on monkfish or lobster for a special occasion, London's fishmongers have the ingredients, knowledge and expertise to make your meal go with a bang. For a jaw-dropping range of fish and shellfish, Golborne Fisheries (see page 97) near Ladbroke Grove is a must, while Mitch Tonk's FishWorks (see page 96) on Marlebone High Street has a traditional wet fish counter as well as a top-class restaurant under one roof.

1 Brown's
2 The Chelsea Fishmonger
3 Covent Garden Fishmongers
4 FishWorks
5 Golborne Fisheries
6 James Knight of Mayfair
7 Moxon's
8 Steve Hatt

Brown's

37-39 Charlbert Street, London NW8 6JN
Tel: 020 7722 8237
Opening times: Mon closed, 8am–5.30pm
Tues–Sat, Sun closed
Tube: St John's Wood

Brown's is a small local fish shop that's tucked away from the main drag of St John's Wood but is still accessible enough to enjoy passing trade and repeat custom. The quality of the fish means that those in the know will willingly slope off from the busier shopping streets to seek the expert advice and enviable knife skills of these helpful fishmongers. Justin and his team will happily de-scale, clean and fillet any of the fish on offer and there's usually a pretty good selection of varieties sourced from all over the world.

Brown's always stocks a wide range, with sustainable wild salmon and tuna being big sellers, as well as daily catches from Cornwall and other parts of the UK and Ireland, such as beautiful Cornish sea bass. You'll find monkfish tails, swordfish, whole squid and smoked trout and there are often specials on the board as well, such as smoked eels and cooked lobster. A range of sauces, soups and other grocery items helps customers to plan a whole meal around whichever variety of fish they choose and the team are only too happy to help with cooking tips for those who want to deviate from their pescatory comfort zone.

While you're in the area...

Panzer's (page 87) is a London institution and worth a visit for its range of grocery and deli goods. If you have time for a stroll, take a detour through Regent's Park then exit the other end and explore the wonderful shops and cafes in and around Marylebone, such as La Fromagerie (page 53), The Ginger Pig (page 37) and The Natural Kitchen (page 112).

The Chelsea Fishmonger

10 Cale Street, London SW3 3QU
Tel: 020 7589 9432
Opening times: Tues–Fri 9-5.30pm, Sat 9am–4pm
Tube: South Kensington or Sloane Square

Rex Goldsmith is about as jovial a shop owner as you could hope to find on a trip out to buy your groceries. He's been running his shop on Cale Street since 2004 but there's been a fishmonger on the site for over 100 years. From his affable manner and enthusiasm for seafood, you'd have no idea that Rex has been up since 4am most mornings, sourcing the best shellfish and smoked fish from Billingsgate Market. The wet fish arrives separately, in a daily delivery from Newlyn Market in Cornwall and the resulting display is diverse and enticing, taking up most of the space at the front of the small shop.

There's Scottish halibut, plaice, whole sides of salmon, mackerel, cod, Dover sole and turbot, as well as dressed crab, smoked cod roe and smoked salmon that comes from a Kosher smoke house just down the road. Rex and his fishmongers know their customers by name and nothing is too much effort; they'll prepare any fish to meet any requirements and no order is too big, too small, or too much effort. It's so refreshing to see people who are genuinely passionate about their work and the food that they source, prepare and sell and The Chelsea Fishmonger is a prime example of this. The tiny shop has a community feel and the friendly banter adds to the shopping experience.

While you're in the area...

The Pie Man is next door and is worthy of its name. If you need something sweet to complement your savoury purchases, pop into Jane Asher, which is also on Cale Street. The expansive Partridges food shop (page 153) is about a ten-minute walk away in Duke of York Square, off King's Road.

Covent Garden Fishmongers

37 Turnham Green Terrace, London W4 1RG
Tel: 020 8995 9273
Opening times: Mon closed, Tues–Weds 8am–5.30pm,
Thurs 8am–5pm, Fri–Sat 8am–5.30pm
Tube: Turnham Green

Although the name suggests otherwise, this longstanding business is actually nowhere near Covent Garden. However, when Philip Diamond first started out, he was selling quality fish and shellfish in the shadow of the Royal Opera House. When they moved to Chiswick the name stuck and the business continued to flourish. I met manager Eddie when I visited the shop and he's been working with Philip and his son, Gary, for over 20 years now. Between them, there's nothing they don't know about fish and they source most of their fresh fish daily from Billingsgate Market, with other varieties coming from Penzance and Iceland.

The shop is stocked with everything a fish lover could possibly require. The fresh fish is gleaming and the selection includes sea bass, skate wing, turbot, lemon sole, salmon, and yellowfin tuna that is of sushi quality. There's also smoked kippers, salmon, trout and whole smoked mackerel, as well as a freezer cabinet packed with prawns, langoustines and stocks. Eddie is keen to get crab back on the British menu so he stocks fresh crabmeat and dressed crab, which is proving popular. A small grocery section includes Stokes sauces, bisques, rouille and aioli, as well as all the makings for a sushi dinner. This is a fishmonger that is completely in tune with the requirements of its customers and it sells exactly what they need, along with a healthy dose of customer service, expertise and a friendly smile.

While you're in the area...

Macken Brothers Ltd is a quality butcher that's just across the road. Theobroma Cacao (page 71)

produces some of the most stunning chocolates in town, and at Mortimer & Bennett delicatessen you'll find a good selection of British and French cheeses and quality groceries.

FishWorks

89 Marylebone High Street, London W1U 4QW
Tel: 020 7935 9796
Opening times: Tues–Sat 10am–10.30pm,
Sun–Mon closed
Tube: Baker Street or Bond Street

This is another string to Marylebone's bow, on a road that positively groans under the weight of quality food shops and eateries. FishWorks has been quietly revolutionising the London fresh fish scene for some time and there are now three branches in the capital. The founder, Mitch Tonks, was spot on when he developed the idea of bringing together the traditional wet fish counter and fish restaurant under one roof. Diners are often so far removed from the food that they're eating that it's difficult to appreciate where it came from, how it was produced and how it was cooked. With the shop on site, customers can see exactly what they'll shortly be eating; indeed they can even choose directly from the display and have their fish cooked to order.

Although the concept isn't unique, the way that this small chain of restaurants has perfected this happy marriage of shop and café puts them at the top of their game. Fish is sourced daily from Cornwall and the gleaming catch-fresh counter offers a great deal of choice to both drop-in customers and diners in the attached restaurant. A range of shellfish, including mussels and cockles, complements the fish and everything in the shop can be prepared to your specific requirements.

Other London branches:
13-19 The Market, The Square, London TW19 1EA
7-9 Swallow Street, London W1B 4DE

While you're in the area...
If you're coming here for lunch, leave some time before or after your reservation to do some food shopping. Natural Kitchen (page 112) is a few shops along the road and is packed full of delectable foodie treats. Turn onto Moxon Street and you'll find cheese heaven in La Fromagerie (page 53) and award-winning meat in The Ginger Pig (page 37).

Golborne Fisheries

77 Golborne Road, London W10 5NL
Tel: 020 8960 3100
Opening hours: Mon closed, Tues–Fri
8.30am–5.30pm, Sat 8.30am–6pm
Tube: Westbourne Park or Ladbroke Grove

If you're a fan of exotic fish and seafood, this is the shop to head for. The vast space is crammed full of fish from all over the world and it's a genuine seafood lover's paradise. There's nothing glamorous or glitzy about the space that has been expanded to accommodate more stock: this is all about the fish. Orders are placed with Billingsgate traders each night, collected early in the morning (that's a fishmonger's early in the morning) and brought back to the shop. There's a vast main counter that groans under the weight of whole fish of varying sizes and you'll always find sea bass, red snapper and red mullet gleaming on their icy beds. You can buy them as seen or ask to have them filleted, the fishmongers are happy to prepare any fish to order.

Keep wandering around and you'll see sardines, scallops, prawns, live clams, live oysters and whelks in one section, as well as crab claw, cockles, crabmeat, kippers and smoked mackerel. Shopping here is an education in itself: aside from Billingsgate Market, I don't think I've seen this many varieties of fish under one roof anywhere else in London. With large Afro-Caribbean, Spanish and Portuguese communities in this part of town, there's definitely a market for such a diverse range of fish and shellfish but, despite the incredible range on display here, everything is fresh, tasty and of exceptional quality.

While you're in the area...

With Portobello Road just a few short steps away, it's no surprise that this is one of the top spots for shopping and eating in town. Le Maroc (page 180) is practically next door and then you can swap Moroccan goodies for Spanish by heading to R. Garcia & Sons (page 182). The Grain Shop is the place to go for bread and Bee Me for honey.

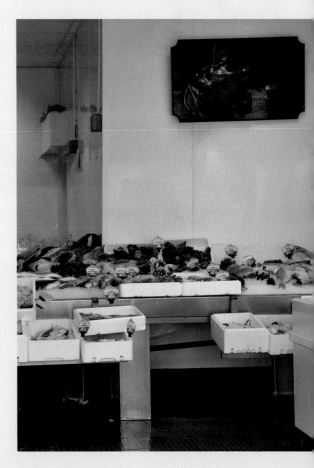

ON ICE

King Prawns.........£20 00
Calamari............£ —
Squid Tubes........£ 695
Baby Squid.........£ —
Whitebait..........£ 4 50
New Zealand Mussels.£ —
Herring Roe........£ 4 80
Breaded Scampi.....£ —
Breaded Plaice Goujons.£ 11 80
Escargot...........£ 4 99
Greenland Prawns (Shell on)..£ 12 50
Mediterranean Prawns...£ 42 00

James Knight of Mayfair

67 Notting Hill Gate, London W11 3JS
Tel: 020 7221 6177
Opening times: Mon–Fri 9am–7.30pm, Sat 9am–6pm
Tube: Notting Hill Gate

I wish I lived closer to this shop as it has everything you could possibly want from a top-quality local fishmonger. The vast, square display is pristine and packed with an abundance of beautiful species of fish and shellfish. There are doors on either side allowing customers maximum vantage points for their purchases, which sit glistening on a thick bed of crushed ice. However, more impressive than all of this is the fact that somewhere in the region of 90% of all the fish sold here is sourced from the UK. James Knight is dedicated to supporting the British fishing industry, as well as cutting down on food miles and encouraging people to eat local, seasonal food. Many people have no idea that fish is seasonal, let alone that much of what's on offer in supermarkets has been flown across the world or has been previously frozen. But Retail Manager, Fiona O'Callaghan and her team hope to change that by stocking the shop with the best of British.

Nothing here is more than 48 hours old so turnaround is quick to ensure the freshness of the fish but the range is impressive too. Cornish sardines, Scottish halibut and scallops, Brixham Dover sole, whelks, razor clams and Irish rock oysters were just some of the varieties on display when I visited. The prices aren't cheap but the absolute guarantee of freshness more than justifies them. The fishmongers know the provenance of every mackerel or clam sold in the shop and their knowledge and knife skills are superlative.

Other London branches:

Selfridges Food Hall, 400 Oxford Street, London W1A 1AB

While you're in the area...

Chegworth Farm Shop (page 147) is just around the corner on Kensington Church Street and you'll have no problems filling a shopping basket here. Head north and there's a whole host of lovely food destinations including The Grocer on Elgin, and the renowned Mr Christian's Deli, also on Elgin Crescent. Finally, find some inspiration for dinner in Books for Cooks on Blenheim Crescent.

Moxon's

149 Lordship Lane, London SE22 8HX
Tel: 020 8299 1559
Opening times: Tues–Sat 9am–5.30pm
Train: East Dulwich

If the unsociable opening hours of Billingsgate are putting you off then you should make a beeline for fishmongers like Moxon's who buy their fish from the venerable market fresh every day. However, they also source certain species direct from suppliers along the South Coast, Cornwall and Scotland to ensure that they supply the best range and quality of fish and seafood to their customers.

The passion and dedication to the fishmonger's craft is obvious as soon as you walk into this shop. The staff are decked out in whiter than white aprons and, when I visited, there was a flurry of activity as whole fish were being expertly boned and filleted to be added to the beautiful display counter. Here, glistening mackerel with bright eyes rest on beds of ice with other popular species such as hake, halibut and lemon sole. But there's plenty to please the more adventurous seafood lover, as well. Rock oysters, live crabs, razor clams, monkfish liver and cod roe are all arranged with such skill and care that it really is difficult to stick to your shopping list.

Moxon's also stock a range of other ingredients to complete your fish supper and a selection of cookery books, if you need a bit of inspiration. But, with so much glorious seafood on offer, a lack of inspiration is highly unlikely.

Other London branches:

Clapham South Underground Station
17 Bute Street, London SW7 3EY

While you're in the area...

Lordship Lane is one long street of quality independent food shops, so run down your larder and get on the train. There's The Cheeseblock (page 49), William Rose butchers (page 45), Green & Blue wine merchants (page 160), SMBS Organic Grocers and the wonderful East Dulwich Deli (page 78).

MOXON'S
SWORDFISH
STEAKS
£17.50 KG

MOXON'S
WILD SEABASS
£15.95 KG

MOXON'S
SALMON FILLET
£14.95 KG

MOXON'S
PLAICE FILLETS

FRESH WILD SALMON TROUT

FRESH RED

Steve Hatt

88-90 Essex Road, London N1 8LU
Tel: 020 7226 3963
Opening times: Mon closed, Tues–Sat
7am–5pm, Sun closed
Tube: Angel

If the awning is down you won't be able to see the shop name but the double-fronted window display of fresh fish and seafood should be a big enough giveaway that you've come to the right address. This utilitarian commercial space is all about the product: there's no fancy décor or plush display cabinets here. The signs are hand-written, many of the fish make do with their polystyrene boxes and any self-respecting interior designer would shudder on stepping inside. But all this is insignificant when you look at the constant stream of customers who are happy to queue for the fantastic range of fresh fish that's sold here. There never seems to be a lull and the fishmongers are kept busy filleting, cleaning and prepping to order, their knives flashing as the ocean's bounty is transformed into dinner party fare.

Mackerel and wild sea bass gleam, while fresh and cooked crabs, Portuguese octopus and live lobsters make up a small selection of the great range of seafood. There's also top-quality smoked salmon and trout, raw prawns and fresh samphire. As word keeps spreading about this fourth-generation fishmonger and his incredible selection of quality seafood, the queues keep getting longer. But nobody seems to mind; it's worth the wait.

While you're in the area...

You're surrounded by good things to eat in this part of town so make a day of it and stock up your shopping bags. Planet Organic (page 113) is a few shops further down Essex Road, whilst award winning chocolatier, Paul A. Young (page 68), weaves his cocoa magic in nearby Camden Passage. Euphorium (page 19) on Upper Street offers a cosy respite and a heady aroma of freshly baked bread.

FOOD HALLS AND EMPORIUMS

There's nothing quite like leisurely wandering around a really well-stocked food hall, looking for some tasty delights, and London surely must have some of the greatest food halls in existence. From the decadece of Harrods' (see page 109) multiple food outlets (which include a cheese counter, a charcouterie and a bakery) and the vast aray of produce on sale at Selfridges (see page 115) to the superior supermarket alternatives that are Planet Organic (see page 113) and Whole Foods Market (see page 120), there's a food hall to suit everyone.

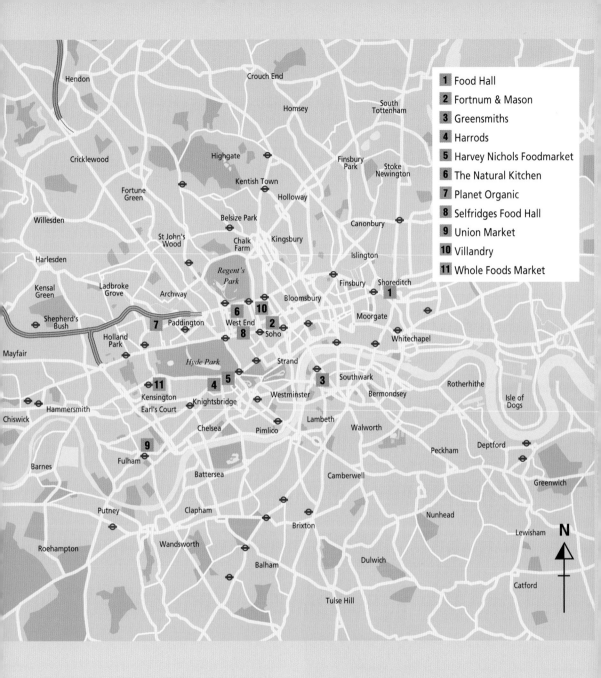

1 Food Hall
2 Fortnum & Mason
3 Greensmiths
4 Harrods
5 Harvey Nichols Foodmarket
6 The Natural Kitchen
7 Planet Organic
8 Selfridges Food Hall
9 Union Market
10 Villandry
11 Whole Foods Market

Food Hall

374-378 Old Street, London EC1V 9LT
Tel: 020 7729 6005
Opening times: Mon–Fri 8.30am–7.15pm,
Sat–Sun 9.30am–5.15pm
Tube: Old Street

Food Hall is a rare find: a superbly well-provisioned shop with a genuinely laid-back vibe. It has been open since 2005 and operates under the ethos of 'slow food with good service'. This was certainly in evidence when I visited. The staff are affable but efficient, which is exactly the right combination for a shop that needs to be able to churn out quality cappuccinos to time-poor office workers, but also spend time explaining products and ingredients to lingering foodies. As soon as you step inside, the clamour of Old Street is washed away and replaced by a sense of calm. The interior is reminiscent of an old-school grocery store, with lots of wood cabinets in muted shades and big tables laden down with goodies. Born and Bread, Flour Power City and Exeter Street Bakery supply fresh loaves, and this level of quality local sourcing extends far beyond the bread counter. The coffee comes from Climpson & Sons, a roastery just down the road in Broadway Market, and when made with creamy milk from Neal's Yard Dairy, it's about as perfect as a coffee can be. I relaxed at one of the tables in the small café area and enjoyed one of the best lattes I've had in a long time.

Neal's Yard also supply the cheese, and varieties such as Stinking Bishop, Vacherin and tangy Morbier share a chilled room with a great selection of fruit and vegetables, and charcouterie such as Proscuitto, Mortadella, salami, and spicy chorizo. Everything in Food Hall seems well thought out and lovingly chosen. A selection of sandwiches and hot meals further emphasises the dedication to quality ingredients and the menu is based on seasonal produce wherever possible.

While you're in the area...

Trendy Shoreditch is a great area to explore, with everything from pop-up fashion shops to high-end hotels and restaurants. Be sure to visit the beautiful Albion café and shop on Boundary Street. You're also just a short walk from the gentrified Arnold Circus, which is home to Leila's Shop, a quirky combination of old-school grocery and laid-back café.

Fortnum & Mason

181 Piccadilly, London W1A 1ER
Tel: 020 7734 8040
Opening times: Mon–Sat 10am–8pm,
Sun 12pm–6pm
Tube: Green Park or Piccadilly Circus

If you receive a Fortnum Christmas hamper you know that someone really loves you. However, whilst it's exciting to open up the wicker treasure trove of foodie delights, it's even better to visit the shop in person and experience the history and elegance of this beautifully appointed grocer. There's nothing like delving around the shelves and counters of outstanding produce to reassure you that food shopping is about so much more than a succession of cling-wrapped barcodes trundling along a conveyor belt.

Fortnum & Mason is steeped in a history that stretches back to its origins as a humble grocery shop in 1707. Though it might have been humble, quality was always at the forefront of its operation. The glamorous food hall certainly oozes elegance now but the insistence on quality remains. From the generously spaced shelves and stands to the lush red carpets and Royal connections, this is really a rather civilised way to buy food. The name itself is a byword for Britishness and, along with Harrods, this is the shop that most tourists tend to make a beeline for, popping tins of loose tea into the eponymous turquoise bags.

Fortnum is indeed famous for its sizable selection of teas but if you slip past the aisles near the entrance or head down the grand staircase, you'll be rewarded with a rich and varied selection of fine foods that have been carefully chosen for their impeccable quality. Smoked fish, meat, cheeses, fresh fruit and vegetables and a sizeable wine collection take up much of the floor space but there's still plenty of room for a cookshop, two restaurants, a café and an ice cream parlour.

While you're in the area...

You can stick with the theme of food halls and head to Selfridges (page 115) on Oxford Street for more visual delights. Or, if your sweet tooth still needs a fix, it's not too far to Charbonnel et Walker (page 64) in The Royal Arcade on Old Bond Street.

Greensmiths

27 Lower Marsh, London SE1 7RG
Tel: 020 7921 2970
Opening time: Mon–Fri 8am–8pm,
Sat 8am–6pm, Sun closed
Tube: Waterloo

If you happen to wander past this neat little shop front, you could be forgiven for thinking it's just a one-room enterprise. But don't be misled by its understated entrance: retrace your steps, go inside and you'll be rewarded with a labyrinth of delicious gourmet treats.

Greensmiths is a fairly recent addition to an area of Waterloo that, for so long, looked a tad tired and forgotten. But with this fantastic collection of independent food retailers all battling for space under one rather small roof, things are definitely on the up. Greensmiths calls itself a 'local supermarket' but it's unlike any high street supermarket you've ever visited. Some of the best names in the independent business have come together to supply customers with a wonderful selection of top-quality food. Think of it as a permanent farmer's market with the bonus of being able to stay dry on rainy days.

The window display is piled high with sausages and pies from The Ginger Pig butcher and this is the first shop within a shop. Next on the culinary tour is The Old Post Office Bakery, with its aromatic range of artisan breads. A little corridor and some winding stairs take you down to Solstice greengrocer, with its abundant fresh fruit and vegetables. These are complemented by a fantastic range of dried goods and grocery staples then it's down another staircase to Waterloo Wine Co. and a lovely little cheese and fresh deli area. They've even managed to make space for a sophisticated mezzanine café, which serves a range of hot and cold food all day.

While you're in the area...

Wander just a few doors down from Greensmiths and you'll come across Café del Marsh. It's a cute little retro coffee shop with great artwork on display. Head across Waterloo Road to the quiet backstreets behind the station and you can marvel at the fresh bread and pastries in Konditor & Cook (page 23). If you fancy a longer walk, you can check out the vast array of quality food shops in and around Borough Market (page 126).

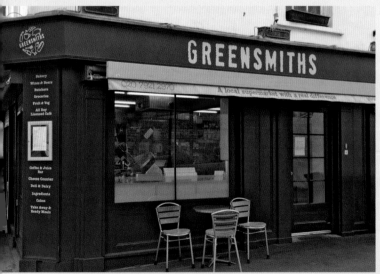

Harrods

87-135 Brompton Road, London SW1X 7XL
Tel: 020 7730 1234
Opening hours: Mon–Sat 10am–8pm, Sun 11.30am–6pm
Tube: Knightsbridge

The fact that Harrods Food Halls are plural should give you some indication of the size and scope of their gourmet offerings. In keeping with everything in this vast store, the food section is truly staggering and there seems to be no end to the rooms, side rooms, counters and eateries that make up this substantial section of the ground floor of the shop. If you begin your tour in the deli room, you'll be bombarded with choice as you walk along the endless cheese counter with its displays of Tomme de Brebis, Morbier, Vacherin and Sussex White Velvet. Keep walking and cheese becomes charcouterie. Here you'll find buffalo firesticks, English biltong, goose ham, ox tongue and pastrami, to name but a few of the vast selection of meats. Next there are filled wraps, pretzels, quiches and pies for lunchtime snacking, through to stuffed poussin, beef

Wellington and lamb en croute for fuss-free evening meals.

Moving through to the produce room, you'll discover shelves of beautiful fresh fruit and vegetables, as well as pantry goods, Wild at Heart flowers and an espresso bar, which you may well need to avail of, if you're to continue on your tour of this gastronomic paradise. Another room is home to the expansive bakery section where loaves, rolls and buns are supplied fresh daily by Paul Hollywood Artisan Bakery Co. Move on again and you can stock up on some Gloucester Old Spot from the butcher counter, fresh bass from the fish counter, or you can sit and enjoy the culinary delights of the Oyster Bar, the Seafood Bar or the Rotisserie. Finally, it's through to tea, coffee and confectionary for some of that eponymous Harrods packaging and a range of chocolate treats from some of the country's finest chocolatiers, including Godiva, Prestat, and Charbonnel & Walker. Now, finally, you can walk out into daylight, blinking like a rabbit in headlights, laden down with gorgeous groceries.

While you're in the area...

A five-minute walk will see you arrive at Harvey Nichols (page 111) for another gastronomic tour. Head a little way south and you can immerse yourself in chocolate magic in Rococo (page 69).

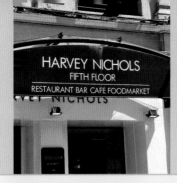

Harvey Nichols Foodmarket

109–125 Knightsbridge, London SW1X 7RJ
Tel: 020 7235 5000
Opening hours: Mon–Sat 10am–8pm, Sun 12pm–6pm
Tube: Knightsbridge

Everyone has heard of Harvey Nichols, many people have visited it but not everyone has made the trip up to the Fifth Floor to peruse the aisles in the Foodmarket. Next time you're in Knightsbridge, set aside some time to come along and have a look. You won't be disappointed with the huge range of eclectic world foods that line the shelves of this large, open-plan space that is flanked by the café and a number of eat-in counters. It's also home to the famous Fifth Floor Restaurant and the chic bar and terrace.

The smell of delicious fresh coffee and cooking food hits you as soon as you exit the lift and you're immediately immersed in a world of classic brands and store-cupboard staples rubbing noses with more unusual finds like Truffle Jam, Poacher's Relish, Rose Nectar, and Pepper Berry and Honey Vinegar. Moving away from the grocery aisles, there's a lovely bread section with loaves provided by Gail's bakery and then a lengthy butcher counter with quality poultry, Scottish Orkney Gold Beef and free-range rare breed pork on display. The deli counter offers everything from olives and dips to Pieminster pies and Dorset ham. The cheese selection changes regularly and includes some of the company's own varieties such as Grana Padano Reserva and Truffle Brie, whilst the fresh fruit and vegetable counter extols the virtues of seasonal British produce as well as exotic favourites from abroad. Foodmarket is an endlessly interesting but relaxed shopping experience, with everything on tap in a spacious but nicely contained space.

While you're in the area...

The immense Food Halls in Harrods (page 109) are well worth a visit but make sure you have no imminent engagements: you might be here for a while. Rococo (page 69) is a chocoholic's treasure trove and you can stop for a coffee while you peruse the laden shelves.

The Natural Kitchen

77-78 Marylebone High Street, London W1U 5JX
Tel: 0203 012 2123
Opening times: Mon–Fri 8am–8pm, Sat 9am–7pm,
Sun 11am–6pm
Tube: Baker Street

The philosophy behind The Natural Kitchen is simple yet impressive: as the name suggests, the food and drink sold here is organic, free range, or artisan produced. There's no space on the counters for factory-farmed meat, pesticide-laden produce or chemically enhanced wine. The layout of The Natural Kitchen is such that it feels like you're shopping in a miniature village high street, populated by a gourmand's dream retail line-up. There's a wonderful deli bar, a small but perfectly formed cheese counter, an off licence section packed with organic wines, and jauntily placed crates of happy-looking vegetables. The butchery counter (Chef & Butcher) brings together the talents of an ex-Chef and a Master Butcher. Together they provide customers with a choice selection of organic and free range meat, as well as cooked dishes such as Salt Marsh Lamb Koftas and Veal Meatballs and more varieties of sausage than you can shake a stick at.

This is food as nature intended and the bustling aisles speak volumes about what customers in this part of town want to buy and are willing to pay a premium for. A store stocked with this benchmark of choice offerings can't begin to compete with the mass production prices of the supermarkets but the quality is superlative, the staff knowledgeable and the actual shopping experience is a total pleasure. There's a wonderful combination of ingredients you actually need to prepare a meal and those that simply look too good to leave behind on the shelf. And when your basket is full and your soul is satiated you can relax in the café for a bowl of homemade soup, a warm sandwich, or a sharing platter.

Other London branches

15-17 Fetter Lane, London EC4A 3AP

While you're in the area...

If your visit to The Natural Kitchen has lit the spark of inspiration, head to Divertimenti on the same road for any kitchen implements you might need to create your masterpiece. Pop round the corner to Moxon Street for the twin delights of La Fromagerie (page 53) and The Ginger Pig (page 37).

Planet Organic

42 Westbourne Grove, London W2 5SH
Tel: 020 7727 2227
Opening times: Mon–Sat 7.30am–9pm,
Sun 12pm–6pm
Tube: Bayswater

Planet Organic offers a viable alternative to supermarket shopping for anyone with a food conscience. With natural, seasonal food as its inspiration, this vast shop manages to retain a sense of community, locality and sensitivity, as well as employing staff who genuinely care about what's in store. I felt instantly energised just by browsing all the healthy and good things to eat and I think that's the key; the food looks wonderfully appetising, the shop is conveniently laid out and there's not an ounce of misplaced worthiness here. The ethos is simple and it centres around the food being natural and wholesome. The meat counter is stocked exclusively with British meat and British seasonal fruit and vegetables take pride of place in the greengrocer section. There are no artificial nasties in the food and the company works closely with its producers

and suppliers to ensure that the staff and buyers know exactly where every last pasta shell and bread roll comes from.

The shop itself is elegant and contemporary with an industrial chic that's softened with bouquets of flowers and the lush displays of fresh food and produce, including a great range of meals to eat in or take out. When I visited, I could choose from a selection including quinoa salad, hot lentil dhal, and spicy bean pie. The grocery section is packed full of cereals, teas, organic pasta and grains, cans, sauces, oils and condiments and the bakery section includes organic spelt, linseed, rye, and traditional soda bread, as well as a number of gluten-free loaves. This really is a one-stop shop for a trolley full of good things and you can also order pretty much everything online as well at planetorganic.com.

Other London branches:

111-117 Muswell Hill Road, London N10 3HS
64 Essex Road, London N1 8LR
22 Torrington Place, London WC1E 7HJ

While you're in the area...

With just a 15-minute walk separating you from Portobello Road, it would be crazy to miss out on the range of great shops in Notting Hill. C. Lidgate (page 31) is one of the best butchers in London, while Mr Christian's on nearby Elgin Crescent is a great local deli.

Selfridges Food Hall

400 Oxford Street, London W1A 1AB

Tel: 0800 123 400

Opening time: Mon–Weds, Fri–Sat 9.30am–8pm,
Thurs 9.30am–9pm, Sun 12pm–6pm

Tube: Bond Street or Marble Arch

If Selfridges is the pinnacle of retail therapy then its substantial food hall is the proverbial icing on the cake. This vast, cavernous space contains more than can be appreciated in just one visit. In fact, unless you have a clear purpose and a purposeful stride you may well stand blinking like a fox in headlights, wondering where to begin your high-end culinary retail crash course.

When you arrive in the food hall, you're initially struck by the almost clinical cleanliness of the sparkling space, the precision shelf stacking and the sheer choice of products, produce and ingredients. There is everything that the discerning (and downright picky) gourmand could possibly desire plus plenty more they didn't even know they wanted. Olive oil has been gathered from the far-flung corners of the world; a whole counter is dedicated to smoked salmon and another to deli delights. Hams hang like attentive doormen and sandwiches are presented like top-end gifts, as opposed to the usual drab low-grade lunch.

Classy concession counters offer a wide range of specialist products, with esteemed fishmonger James Knight dealing with seafood requirements, Jack O'Shea providing meat, and Turnips the grocer selling fresh fruit and vegetables. If you want to eat in, there's even more choice and it comes down to whether you want to linger at a table or park your bottom on a bar stool. Square Pie and Tiffin Bites offer quality fast food, while the Oyster & Champagne Bar elevates the traditional shopping break to another level. And when you've got your breath back, you can head back into the throng: from breakfast cereal to buffalo biltong, there's not a lot you can't buy here.

While you're in the area...

Escape the hustle and bustle of Oxford Street and take a more sedate stroll around Mayfair. You can pop into Allens (page 30) on Mount Street to see a traditional butcher at work, or check out the gorgeous little Mount Street Deli a few doors further down the road.

Union Market

472 Fulham Road, London SW6 1BY
Tel: 020 7386 2470
Opening times: Mon–Fri 7am–10pm, Sat–Sun 9am–9pm
Tube: Fulham Broadway

Union Market is a rare find for anyone who's looking for convenience but also has concerns about supporting British food producers and not relying on supermarkets for their weekly shop. I like shopping here for all these reasons but also because the shopping experience itself is enjoyable. Union Market is set up much like a traditional shopping street or market, with demarcated areas for different foods, all of which lead naturally to each other and are all under one

roof. The huge domed space has light pouring in from the vast glass ceiling and gives the impression of walking down a Victorian high street, with a bakery, a butcher, a greengrocer and a fishmonger all lined up ready for your custom. It's spacious and interesting with traditional signs and fittings combined with modern styling to create a unique retail area.

The shop is true to its mission statement and largely stocks British produce. Bread is supplied by Bread Factory, cheese by Neal's Yard Dairy and meat and poultry is exclusively British. Even the fruit and vegetables are largely chosen on the basis of being seasonal and British. Small, independent producers have been brought on board to showcase the quality and extent of British food and it's refreshing to see this level of research and dedication to British indigenous food in the centre of London. Whilst no one wants to wax lyrical about British food to the detriment of choice produce from abroad, it's important to offer it on a large scale in order to demonstrate the sheer range of home-grown goodies we have on our doorstep and Union Market is a champion for the cause.

While you're in the area...

Head to Del Aziz on Vanston Place for the best in Mediterranean and Middle Eastern food. There's a large deli section, a bakery and a café for more leisurely eating. Vagabond wine merchants (page 171) is next door to the deli and this concept store allows you to taste from a wide selection of wines, before making your final decision.

Villandry

170 Great Portland Street, London W1W 5QB
Tel: 020 7631 3131
Opening times: Mon–Sat 8am–10pm, Sun 9am–4pm
Tube: Great Portland Street or Oxford Circus

There's a certain amount of passing trade in Villandry but you get the impression that most of the shoppers and diners in this elegant emporium haven't arrived here by accident. The distinctive green awnings along the lengthy shop front alert you to the fact that you're about to enter one of the best food stores in London and, once inside, it's difficult to decide where to begin.

Villandry is a veritable cornucopia of food treats and it manages to successfully embrace its many roles of delicatessen, bakery, bar and restaurant with effortless professionalism. The dizzying selection of charcouterie, bread, choice deli fare, fresh produce, dried food, wine and confectionery can make for a lengthy shop but filling a basket here is all pleasure and no chore. The edibles are complemented by an eclectic selection of gifts, trinkets and books: a balanced mix of serious and fun food-related paraphernalia.

If you need a break from the food shelves, there's a range of options for sampling the food. Busy office workers queue at the deli counter for freshly prepared salads and sandwiches; those with a longer lunch break take a seat in the bar; and those with no time constraints head to the restaurant. Service is slick throughout the store, with staff in starched aprons bustling to and fro with everything from freshly baked bread and freshly brewed coffee to a whole grilled lemon sole. If you can find a vacant chair in the bar area (and there's a big 'if' here), put the next half an hour on hold and watch the heart of Villandry beat.

Other London branches

95-97 High Holborn, London WC1V 6LF (Villandry Kitchen)
219-221 Chiswick High Road (Villandry Kitchen)

While you're in the area...

Marylebone High Street is a brisk ten minutes' walk away with its vast array of fine food shops, including La Fromagerie (page 53), The Ginger Pig (page 37) and The Natural Kitchen (page 112).

Whole Foods Market

63-97 Kensington High Street, London W8 5SE
Tel: 020 736 8450
Opening times: Mon–Sat 8am–10pm, Sun 12pm–6pm
Tube: High Street Kensington

If you ever use the excuse that supermarket shopping is more convenient, you probably don't live close to a Whole Foods Market. Admittedly, the Kensington branch is by far the biggest but with regards to product range and choice, it can rival any branded supermarket any day of the week. The difference here is that every single item on the shelves has been rigorously sourced to ensure its provenance. The food here is free from artificial preservatives, flavours and sweeteners, and the emphasis is on natural and organically grown foods.

Whole Foods is a household name in its home country of America but in the UK we're still getting used to the fact that healthy, organic, free range and whole foods can make up the entirety of a food cupboard and a trolley full of the good stuff needn't break the bank. You really can buy everything here and the tour begins with a large bakery as you enter on the ground floor. When you move into the main shopping area, you'll discover lengthy counters of freshly prepared salads, vegetable dishes, mix and match pastas and sauces, and rice dishes to take away. There are also 'Ready to Cook' sections where freshly prepared meals like crab cakes, chicken Parmesan, and sweet potato and quinoa cakes can all be picked up for your evening meal.

The shelves are all incredibly well stocked and the sections well defined and easy to navigate. A large wine and beer aisle leads over to the immense cheese area that consists of both a counter and a dedicated cheese room, which puts other shops to shame. On the deli counter, Wild boar, Speck and Chorizo de Bellota all demand attention but this is just a small sample of the meat available in store. Go downstairs and you'll find one of the biggest butcher counters in town, where the meat is clearly labelled with its origin and even the name of the farm in some cases. There's dry-aged beef, veal, lamb noisettes and sausages that are made fresh every day. The fish counter gleams with fresh tilapia fillets, sea bass and squid rings whilst the endless rows of nuts, seeds, dried fruit, lentils, rice and pasta are incredible. This vast emporium is crammed full of healthy goodies and it really is a pleasure to shop here. And, once the shopping is done, you can head upstairs to a choice of restaurants and cafes serving food from around the world.

Other London branches:

305–311 Lavender Hill, London SW11 1LN
69–75 Brewer Street, London W1F 9US
32–40 Stoke Newington Church Street, London N16 0LU

While you're in the area...

Keep walking along Kensington High Street until you reach Hotel Chocolat (page 66) with its sumptuous displays of all things cocoa-related. If you need a sit down and a nice cup of tea, you should check out The Muffin Man Tea Shop on nearby Wright's Lane for a retro cuppa and cake.

FOOD AND FARMERS' MARKETS

Farmers' Markets have become incredibly popular in London in recent years as more and more city-dwellers look to artisan and locally-produced produce. What London lacks in farms it certainly makes up for in good-quality food markets. Most areas now have at least one local food market, and here you'll find a selection of the biggest and the best. Borough Market (see page 126) is without doubt the most well known of the capital's food markets, and if you only visit one, make it this one. Billingsgate Market (see page 124) is an absolute must, not only for its astounding selection of fish and shellfish, but also for the wonderful experience of wandering the isles at the crack of dawn and soaking up the atmosphere.

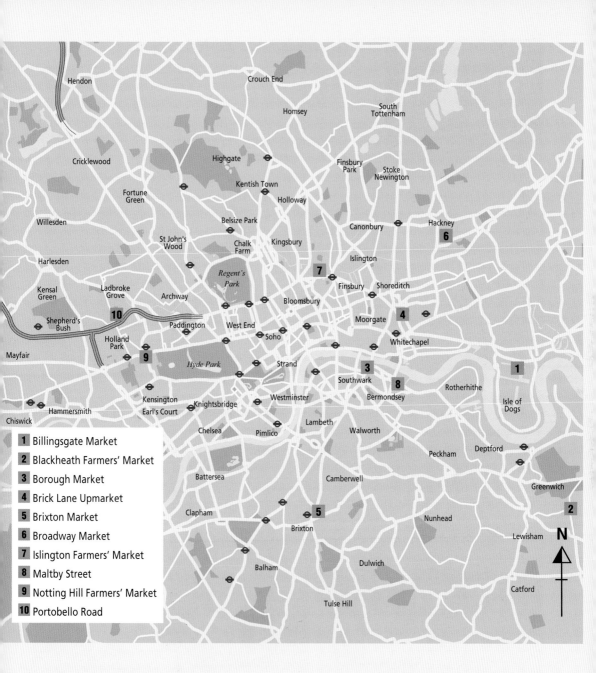

Hendon
Crouch End
Homsey
South Tottenham
Cricklewood
Highgate
Finsbury Park
Stoke Newington
Kentish Town
Holloway
Fortune Green
Belsize Park
Canonbury
Hackney **6**
Willesden
St John's Wood
Chalk Farm
Kingsbury
Islington
Harlesden
Regent's Park
7
Kensal Green
Ladbroke Grove
Archway
Finsbury
Shoreditch
Bloomsbury
Moorgate
4
Shepherd's Bush
10
Paddington
West End
Soho
Whitechapel
Holland Park
Mayfair
9
Hyde Park
Strand
1
Kensington
3
Southwark
Chiswick
Earl's Court
Knightsbridge
Westminster
Bermondsey
8
Rotherhithe
Hammersmith
Chelsea
Pimlico
Lambeth
Walworth
Isle of Dogs
Battersea
Camberwell
Peckham
Deptford
Greenwich
Clapham
5
Nunhead
Brixton
Lewisham
2
Balham
Dulwich
Catford
Tulse Hill

1 Billingsgate Market
2 Blackheath Farmers' Market
3 Borough Market
4 Brick Lane Upmarket
5 Brixton Market
6 Broadway Market
7 Islington Farmers' Market
8 Maltby Street
9 Notting Hill Farmers' Market
10 Portobello Road

N

Billingsgate Market

Trafalgar Way, London E14 5ST
Tel: 020 7987 1118
Opening times: Tues-Sat 5am-8.30am,
Sun-Mon closed (also closed Tues after
Bank Holiday Mondays)
Tube: Canary Wharf or Blackwall DLR

You'll need to be dedicated to your fish and seafood to make the early call for this market. Everything starts to wind down at about 8am but most of the serious trading is done well before this, so if you want to immerse yourself in centuries of history then you'll have to set your alarm clock. If you do make the effort to traipse across town to this massive warehouse in the middle of Docklands, you'll be mightily rewarded. The cacophony of sound, the barrage of smells and the genuinely exhilarating market experience will ensure that the sleep is banished from your eyes as soon as you walk in.

Billingsgate is primarily a wholesale market but that's not to say it's out of bounds to individual food fanatics: you just need to buy in bulk. So, clear out your freezer before you go and bag yourself a bargain box of freshly caught bass or some melt-in-the-mouth Arbroath Smokies. As you wander around, you'll see hundreds of species of familiar and exotic fish and shellfish with serious buyers sniffing, prodding and closely inspecting the displays. There's no holds barred here; this is a million miles away from the fixed prices and genteel pleasantries of Central London farmers' markets. In Billingsgate, voices are raised as buyers and traders each try to bag themselves the best deal.

I researched the history of the market for a book a few years ago, so I've spent a number of mornings pacing the market floor, dodging the porters' trolleys and listening to the tales of the traders. Although I might be slightly biased, this is, without doubt, one of my favourite London food markets. It's a truly unique experience that is well worth a few hours' lost sleep.

While you're in the area...

You'll probably leave the market before most people have left their houses for work. Luckily, Billingsgate is just a stone's throw from Canary Wharf, where round-the-clock hours mean early opening times for shops and cafes. Check out Charbonnel et Walker (page 64) for a sweet diversion, or head to Square Pie for a more substantial savoury snack.

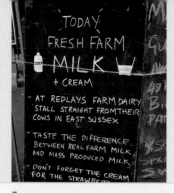

Blackheath Farmers' Market

Blackheath Station car park, London, SE3 9LA
Opening times: Sun 10am–2pm
Train: Blackheath

It may not be the biggest market or have the most number of stalls but it is one of the original London Farmers' Markets and, as such, has built up a loyal local following. With no supermarket in the centre of Blackheath, this market really does provision a lot of local larders and people come here to shop rather than just browse, prod, inspect and smell. As with all the markets that are run under this scheme, producers do vary each week and you rarely get exactly the same line up. However, there are plenty who turn up as regularly as clockwork and these are the stalls with the queues. When I come here, I always buy a pugliese loaf from Exeter Street Bakery, broccoli quiches and chocolate brownies from Artisan Foods and eggs from Harvest Moon. That's by no means the full extent of my shopping bag; the rest depends on what looks good on the day.

Like many local food markets, Blackheath has made the most of a space that is rarely used at the weekends and stalls are set up in the train station car park. Other markets around London make use of school playgrounds, office car parks or quiet side streets and it's great to see these bland and featureless spaces coming alive with the sights, sounds and smells of market life. In Blackheath, the central location ensures it really is an important part of the ebb and flow of village life and all the nearby cafes spill over with market shoppers and their bags laden down with bread and vegetables.

London Farmers' Markets:

At the time of writing there were 18 London Farmers' Markets and all of these are Certified by FARMA (National Farmers' Retail and Markets Association). To be Certified, market producers must come from within 100 miles of the M25 and they have to raise, grow or bake everything they sell. This ensures that quality is paramount and, for their part, the producers get a fair price for all their hard work. To find out more, go to www.farmersmarkets.net.

While you're in the area...

If the sun is out, stock up on goodies from the market and head to the Heath for a picnic. Once you've finished, keep walking over the Heath and through Greenwich Park then reward yourself with a coffee and cake in Paul Rhodes bakery (page 27). If the weather isn't playing ball, stay in Blackheath and pop into Handmade Food on Tranquil Vale for an award-winning snack or meal.

Borough Market

8 Southwark Street, London SE1 1TL
Tel: 020 7407 1002
Opening times: Thurs 11am–5pm,
Fri 12pm–6pm, Sat 8am–5pm
Tube: London Bridge or Borough

This is without doubt, the most well known and, many would argue, best food market in London. With literally hundreds of stalls selling top-quality artisan food, there really is something for everyone in this sprawling expanse of high-end food consumerism under the railway viaducts at London Bridge. So much has been written about this bastion of gastronomy that it's almost impossible to add a new angle or any new information. If you've been, you know how fantastic it is, if you haven't then why not for heaven's sake?

Chefs, tourists, local residents, food voyeurs, food snobs, bargain hunters, connoisseurs, dating couples, harried families, solvent singles, dinner party hosts, carnivores, vegetarians and endless amateur photographers pass through the market every weekend and space becomes limited as the halls fill up. The air is scented with sizzling wild breed sausages and burgers, freshly baked bread and freshly ground coffee, while sellers offer morsels of everything from mozzarella cheese to spicy chorizo sausages to passing customers. Traders such as Flour Power City, Furness Fish & Game and Turnips grocery have a loyal clientele who return each week for quality sourdough or new season fruit and vegetables. Other, smaller stalls rely on passing trade and word-of-mouth recommendations.

Aside from the stalls, you'll find a number of permanent shops in and around the market and these often have daily opening hours. Applebees Fish is a fantastic combination of fresh fish counter and café, and Rabot Estate is a chocoholics dream with varieties such as dark chilli, pistachio, and

coffee bean, as well as a range of chocolate-based drinks and snacks.

While you're in the area...

To be honest, if you've spent a morning shopping in Borough Market you probably need a sit down and a back rub instead of more walking. If you can't find what you're looking for here, you probably won't find it anywhere. But, if your feet and your purse can handle it, Maltby Street Market (page 136), Bermondsey Street and Shad Thames are all fairly close by and each offers even more foodie treats.

Brick Lane Upmarket

Ely's Yard, The Old Truman Brewery, London E1 6QL
Tel: 020 7770 6028
Opening times: Sun 10am–5pm
Tube: Aldgate East or Liverpool Street

Sunday Upmarket is evocative of the Brick Lane area in general: vibrant, eclectic and innovative with equal doses of shabby and chic. Although much of the Truman Brewery has now been transformed into designer office suites for media companies, the market hall remains un-gentrified and resembles a disused aircraft hangar. However, its charm undoubtedly lies in its disarray and if you're looking for a more genteel experience, you're just a few minutes from the stunningly redeveloped Spitalfields Market.

Upmarket boasts a huge range of stalls that covers the gamut from hand printed T-shirts to handmade cupcakes and pretty much anything else in between. Independent clothes and jewellery designers have the opportunity to showcase their designs and the whole hall buzzes with traders and customers selling and buying unique pieces. The mish-mash of stalls operates against a mash-up of music from the various stereos pumping out genre-defying tunes and you need to wrestle your way to

the back of the hall to reach the food area. The smells will help to guide you and your mouth will be watering long before you reach the first portable kitchen. There is freshly made hot food from virtually every corner of the globe and it takes a good few turns of the stalls to narrow down your lunch choice. Turkish fusion, Sri Lankan curry, Chinese noodles, Thai snacks, Belgian waffles, Caribbean chicken, Ethiopian beef, sushi, falafel, halal, vegan, the list goes on. My masala potatoes and garlic chicken roti roll was a difficult decision to make but a good one.

While you're in the area...

Pop inside the Truman Brewery for the Boiler House, a new food market with an international flavour. Check out the rest of the quirky shops and diverse range of eateries on Brick Lane. Alternatively, wander a few minutes' south and you'll reach Spitalfields with its vast indoor market space. This area is also home to some notable food shops like Montezuma's (page 67) and A. Gold (page 144).

BRIXTON FOODLAND
VARIETY OF FOOD & GROCERIES
AFRO-CARIBBEAN FOOD-SPECIALIST
6 market row
SUPERMALT
BANAMIEL
Jelly 1.50 EACH
COLOMBA CHOW CHOW

Brixton Market

Electric Avenue, London SW9 8JX
Tel: 07960 942060
Opening times: Mon-Tues 8am–6pm,
Weds 8am–3pm, Sat 8am–6pm, Sun
10am–2pm (farmers' market)
Tube: Brixton

Brixton Market is a sprawling, all-encompassing and incredibly diverse shopping area that's open for business throughout the week, although certain days are dedicated to different stalls. The food on sale here reflects the ethnic diversity of the area and this is one of the best spots in London for African and Caribbean produce and ingredients. Brixton Market isn't one contained area; there are lots of individual facets to explore. The main outdoor market runs along Electric Avenue, so named because it was the first street market to have electric lighting. It's here that you'll find the incredible range of exotic fruit and vegetables that the market is famous for and this is the place to really soak up the unique atmosphere of Brixton. Once you've filled a shopping bag or two head inside one of the market arcades.

The entrance to Brixton Village is fairly unassuming but go inside and you'll discover over 100 shops so make sure you're blocked out your diary for the day if you want to do some serious browsing. There's plenty more food, including exotic fish from the Caribbean, speciality dried fish, and Asian, West Indian and European foods, ingredients, herbs and spices. There's also an ever-changing collection of pop-up shops and boutiques, selling everything from handbags to jewellery. Head around the corner to Market Row and you'll discover another traditional arcade crammed full of eclectic shops and cafes, including the wonderful Rosie's Deli Café.

While you're in the area...

While you're at the market, check out some of the shops as well. Breads etc opened in Brixton Arcade in 2010 and has made a name for itself with its quality bread. Continental Delicatessen sells a wonderful array of herbs, spices, cheese and meat.

Broadway Market

London Fields, London E8
Opening times: Sat 9am–5pm
Tube: Hackney Central

Broadway market is a local institution, having been proffering its wares to savvy shoppers since the 1890s. If you want to fully appreciate the diversity of London's food markets then you should make a beeline for Hackney and this eclectic but largely traditional community market. For a first-timer, it can be a bit overwhelming, especially if you're more used to the finite selections and less numerous stalls at the small but perfectly formed farmers' markets around the capital. But you go to Broadway as much for the atmosphere as the shopping and this market is so steeped in East End traditions that a stroll through this vast and bustling marketplace is like taking a crash course in local history.

The market has survived a turbulent history, which saw its slow demise in the eighties and nineties, followed by a meteoric about turn in fortunes that reflects the gritty East End character. The whole community was revitalised by the Broadway Market Traders' and Residents' Association in 2004 and its now a destination shopping area. There are more than 80 stalls in the market and you can expect to find everything from East End barrow boys selling a huge range of fresh fruit and vegetables, to meat and fish stalls and a great variety of fresh bread and pastries. There are also cakes, a global selection of enticing hot snacks, good coffee, quality cheese and a random collection of non-food stalls. The market is at the centre of proceedings but there are also an increasing number of independent shops and cafes lining the street. These include Climpsons Café, and Cookes, which has been serving pie and mash and jellied eels for over 100 hundred years. History and modernity happily co-exist in Broadway Market and it should be on everyone's food to-do list.

While you're in the area...

Once you've wondered through the expansive market, head towards Victoria Park and you can taste a selection of wines before you buy at Bottle Apostle (page 159). Ginger Pig (page 37) also has a shop on Lauriston Road.

PEPPER

WILD BOAR

SMOKED

Islington Farmers' Market

Chapel Market, London N1 9PZ
Tel: 020 7833 0338
Opening times: Sun 10am–2pm
Tube: Angel

This area of Islington is no stranger to market stalls with a daily street market on the road, which can be heard long before it's seen. However, on Sunday it's the turn of the weekly Farmers' Market to take over the space and this delightful addition to the shopping options of Angel has become a foodie destination.

This was the first market opened by London Farmers' Markets, which now run 18 markets around the capital, all of which adhere to its set criteria to ensure quality for the consumer. With over 30 stalls towards the Penton Street end of Chapel Market, this is one of the largest Farmers' Markets in London and it's always busy. There's a good range of free range and organic meat on offer from numerous suppliers, including Beatbush Farm Foods and Downland Pigs. There's Lincolnshire Poacher Cheese and other dairy delights from FW Read and Son, and Celtic Bakers and Flour Power City make bread lovers happy. Ted's Veg are a welcome presence at many markets and their range of seasonal produce is second-to-none. The Pudding Shop is a St Albans-based artisan bakery using organic flour to produce the incredible range of classic puds such as treacle sponge, and bread and butter pudding. With such a diverse range of suppliers and produce, it's easy to see why this longstanding market is still a London favourite.

While you're in the area...

You're right in the heart of Islington here, so take the opportunity to pop into the likes of Paul A. Young (page 68) for upmarket chocolates, Euphorium (page 19) for delicious bread and The Sampler (page 167) for a wide range of wine.

Maltby Street

Maltby Street, Druid Street, Stanworth Street, The Rope Walk, SE1
Opening times: Sat 9am–2pm
Tube: London Bridge or Bermondsey

Since it first opened in September 2010, this collection of food purveying railway arches has gained a steady following, predominantly amongst those who are fed up with jostling the crowds in Borough Market. It began as an experiment but has become a regular fixture for foodies who want to do serious shopping. In theory, the idea of opening a market so close to the mighty Borough might seem laughable, but in practise the gamble has paid off and this little enclave of arches scattered around the less salubrious backstreets of Bermondsey is becoming a destination in its own right.

The cavernous arches are dotted throughout a number of roads around Maltby Street. If you begin your visit at Monmouth Coffee Company (34 Maltby Street), you can work your way around the other producers here and on The Rope Walk, Stanworth Street and Druid Street, then end up back where you started, having completed a glorious gourmand loop. During the week, many of the arches are storehouses, production units and warehouses for the suppliers who trade from them so it was a small but perfectly natural leap to open them up for retail purposes on a Saturday.

Despite the rather stark, industrial backdrop, the atmosphere here is laid back and there's ample opportunity for producers and customers to interact. KaseSwiss offers the best in Swiss cheese, while in Boerenkaas you can sample wonderful Dutch farmhouse cheeses like the stunning Young Remeker, and over in Booth's there's pretty much all the fruit and vegetables you could ask for. At Fern Verrow (55 Stanworth Street) you can buy biodynamic vegetables direct from the farm and St John Bakery (72 Druid Street) sells a selection of its renowned loaves and pastries. With more producers expressing an interest in setting up shop under the arches, Maltby Street is set to get even bigger and better in the future.

While you're in the area...

Depending on whether you've come here to avoid Borough Market or complement it, you may or may not want to continue your foodie expedition to the better-known SE1 food market. Otherwise, Shad Thames is a short walk away and the Wine Cellar and Foodstore at Le Pont de la Tour are well worth visiting.

Notting Hill Farmers' Market

Car Park Behind Waterstone's, Kensington Church Street, London W11 3PB
Tel: 020 7833 0338
Opening times: Sat 9am–1pm
Tube: Notting Hill Gate

If you were to wander around Notting Hill on a Saturday you could quite easily miss this well-established market. It's tucked away in a little car park behind the corner of Notting Hill Gate and Kensington Church Street. It's no great surprise that locals are keen to keep their secret as the area is often under siege from tourists loved up on the back of a certain film. Its obscurity has done nothing to hinder its success however, and the place is buzzing with foodies loading up linen bags with bundles of farm fresh veggies, quality meats, farmhouse cheeses and more bread than you can, well, shake a breadstick at.

The market is part of the London Farmers' Markets scheme, which ensures authenticity, genuine local produce and strict criteria for producers to adhere to. Many stallholders are here every week, which I think is important for building up a truly loyal following and encouraging people to do some serious shopping, with lists in hand. When I visited,

Flourish bakery had a stall, as did Nut Knowle Farm, and the wonderful Olive Farm who produce some wonderfully tasty cheese and other dairy products. There was also organic veg, homemade pies, and beautiful ready-to-eat Italian dishes from Seriously Italian. Chegworth Valley Juices have a stall but they've also got a whole farm shop that backs onto the market and sells a wide range of produce and foods from their own and other local farms. This market has a genuine local feel to it but the food is seriously good and the choice makes it a worthy detour if you're elsewhere in town.

While you're in the area...

You're quite literally on the doorstep of Chegworth Farm Shop (page 147) and it's well worth a browse. Escape the hustle and bustle of Notting Hill Gate and pay & Clarke's (page 15) a visit, it's one of the most beautiful bakeries you'll ever visit.

The Royal Borough of Kensington and Chelsea
PORTOBELLO ROAD, W.11.

Portobello Road

Portobello Road, London, W10
Opening times (fruit and vegetable market):
Mon–Weds 8am–6.30pm, Fri–Sat 8am–6.30pm
Tube: Notting Hill Gate

As one of London's most famous markets, Portobello Road certainly has a big reputation to live up to. Luckily, it succeeds on every count and is well deserving of its fame. The road is probably best known for the weekly antiques market, which takes place every Saturday and attracts dealers and buyers from all over the country. This is without doubt the busiest day but visit on any other day of the week and you'll find things a little less frenetic and a little more low-key. There are a number of sections within this sprawling stretch of market stalls that runs the full length of the road but the main fruit and veg section is around Elgin Crescent and you'll find stalls here every day selling a wide range of fresh produce.

Although the food offering is mainly destined for the fruit bowl and the vegetable rack, you'll also find a fishmonger, and some quality cheese and bread amongst the barrows. Move in one direction or another and you'll come across household goods, second-hand clothes, new clothes and the odd smattering of furniture and knick-knack stalls. Of course, no one travels to Portobello Road just for the fruit stalls; it's all about atmosphere here and it really is a lovely part of London. With its eclectic and diverse range of delis, shops, cafes and restaurants, with a truly cosmopolitan feel, it's possible to arrive for breakfast and eat and shop your way around the world without leaving Portobello Road. By dinnertime you'll be replete, exhausted, lighter of wallet and heavier of shopping bag but seriously food happy.

While you're in the area...

Coffee Plant is just one of many great cafes in the area, and Golborne Fisheries (page 97) offers an incredible range of exotic fish and seafood. Mr Christian's on Elgin Crescent is one of the best delis in the neighbourhood and next door Jeroboam's (page 161) is a wine connoisseur's haven.

GROCERS AND FARM SHOPS

Grocers shops where once the stalwart of most high-streets, until sadly many were forced to close as trade was lost to large supermarkets. However recent years have seen the local grocer thrive once again and the capital has a marvellous variety of excellent grocers and farm shops. Kentish Town is home to the wonderfully-named Bumblebee Natural Foods (see page 145), specialising in natural, organic and vegetarian produce. While visitors to and inhabitants of west London are blessed with the delightful Chegworth Farm Shop (see page 147) with its links to the Chegworth Valley fruit farm in Kent. It really is a little piece of the countryside right here in London.

1 A. Gold
2 Bumblebee Natural Foods
3 Chegworth Farm Shop
4 Daylesford Organic
5 Franklins Farm Shop
6 Highgate Village Fruiterers
7 Michanicou Bros
8 Partridges
9 Yeomans

A. Gold

42 Brushfield Street, London E1 6AG
Tel: 020 7247 2487
Opening times: Mon–Fri 10am–4pm, Sat–Sun 11am–5pm
Tube: Liverpool Street, Aldgate East

If there's a food shop in London that proves the theory that size isn't everything, then this is it. Spatially challenged it might be, but the quirky range of hard-to-find products makes it a worthwhile destination. A. Gold is a proponent of quality British foodstuffs and this is indeed an enclave of Britishness, calling itself a 'village shop in the city'. It's an apt description because walking into A. Gold is like stepping back in time to a traditional grocery store; a place where you'd buy a pound of loose leaf tea, a quarter of lemon bonbons and a nice piece of

cake. Many of the products sold here are unique to this shop and people do travel here especially for items like Campbells tea. Whilst here, they might also pop some mushroom ketchup, coconut ice, Gentlemen's Relish, honeycomb or pickled eggs in their basket. There's always something new on the shelves and this randomness is all part of the charm.

As with many small businesses in Spitalfields, A. Gold has adapted, and the shop now offers the increasing number of city workers in the area a range of top-notch sandwiches, including a daily hot special. A tiny table at the back of the shop allows nimble footed customers with eagle eyes to eat-in, whilst the rest can watch their lunch being prepared at a wooden table piled high with ingredients that make these sandwiches worth travelling for. But for me, it's the scotch eggs, halved and smeared with eye-watering mustard that will keep me going back.

While you're in the area...

Verde & Co is a small grocer and deli next door to A. Gold and the two are perfectly matched for a foodie outing. The owner, Harvey Cabaniss, was a chef until he started the business in 2004 and he has created a gorgeous shop that is stocked with all his favourite foods, including the award-winning chocolates of Pierre Marcolini. Each day Harvey and his team create a couple of hot dishes using ingredients from local producers. The day I stopped by, they were busy serving shoulder of pork with beans to a queue of regulars. Ad hoc seasonal and speciality fruit and vegetables are often for sale too in this delightful little refuge in the heart of Spitalfields.

Bumblebee Natural Foods

30-32 Brecknock Road, London N7 0DD
Tel: 020 7284 1314
Opening times: Mon-Sat 9am-6.30pm
Tube: Kentish Town

This collection of shops is a real find and, as far as I'm aware, unique in London. Bumblebee Natural Foods is actually three individual shops on Brecknock Road. Two are next to each other, whilst the greengrocer is across the road. The owner, Iain, explained that this quirky set-up came about because they wanted to expand the business and took on the extra premises when they became available. Although he spends much of his time crossing the road and opening and shutting doors, Iain is happy with the current configuration and the shops are so defined that customers know exactly where to go for everything they need.

The grocery – or provisions – shop is the original Bumblebee and it's here that you'll find a fantastic selection of nuts, dried fruit, jam, chutney and local honey as well as everything else you might need to stock an organic larder. Natural, organic and vegetarian produce and ingredients are at the heart of the business but there's a big emphasis on keeping a wide range of stock and ensuring everything is reasonably priced, making it a viable choice for a weekly shop. The bakery is next door and it's stocked with a wide range of bread, including spelt and gluten-free loaves. It's also here that you can buy hot meals and the kitchen cooks up a daily changing menu of three dishes, as well as homemade soup, flans, quiche, pastries and salads. Cross the road and you'll find the greengrocers, stocked with crates of fresh organic fruit, vegetables and salad leaves. There's a small but perfectly formed dairy counter at the back with cheese, milk, yogurt and butter and there's also a good range of ethical cleaning products.

While you're in the area...

While you're on Brecknock Road, check out Salvino Delicatessen for a great range of Italian ingredients. If you're travelling back via Kentish Town, Harry's Fine Foods is just opposite the station and is a one-stop shop for meat and fish.

Chegworth Farm Shop

221 Kensington Church Street, London W8 7LX
Tel: 020 7229 3016
Opening times: Mon–Fri 8am-9pm, Sat 8am–8pm,
Sun 9am–6pm
Tube: Notting Hill Gate

Farm shops can take on all manner of incarnations in central London but walking into Chegworth really is like stepping inside a well-stocked produce barn in the middle of Kent: you wouldn't feel out of place here in your wellies and Barbour. That's not to say it's haphazard or randomly stocked: far from it, it's just that this shop is authentic. And there's a very good reason for this authenticity. Charlotte is the manageress and her parents own Chegworth Valley fruit farm, which is indeed in Kent and has long been associated with the outstanding fruit juices that are made from their apples and pears. Whilst they still predominantly sell their fruit and juices at farmers' markets and via other outlets, the shop is a wonderful addition to the business, and it gives the family the opportunity to sell their own, and other organic farmers', produce to appreciative customers.

The food in the shop is local and seasonal and there's a delivery from Chegworth Valley every morning to replenish the shelves with some of the freshest produce you're likely to buy anywhere nearby. Other local organic farms fill any gaps in the shelves ensuring a constant supply of farm fresh veggies and salad leaves all year round. There are also plenty of groceries on offer, including granola, eggs, farmhouse cheeses, ready meals, eggs, yogurt and milk, as well as honey, chutney and jam, which are made on the farm. Variety, quality and freshness make this emporium a one-stop shop.

While you're in the area...

Pop round the corner to James Knight of Mayfair (page 99) on Notting Hill Gate for a stunning selection of British fish and seafood. Or, cross the road and sample fresh bread and pastries in the gorgeously appointed & Clarkes bakery (page 15). You can keep giving into your sugar cravings at The Cupcake Company on Kensington Church Street, where the gorgeous creations are too irresistible to walk past.

Daylesford Organic

44b Pimlico Road, London SW1W 8LP
Tel: 020 7881 8060
Opening times: Mon–Sat 8am–7pm, Sun
10am–4pm
Tube: Sloane Square

This is a beautiful shop selling beautiful food and it really is a joy to visit. On sunny days the windows by the full-length eat-in counter are thrown open and the shop is bathed in light and the hum of convivial conversation. The interior is a gloriously spacious layout of marble floors and counters, interspersed with stand-alone displays decked out with wicker baskets of glossy fruit and vegetables and aromatic bread including sourdough, pumpernickel, and Danish rye.

All the fresh, seasonal produce and meat in the shop has been raised or grown on the farm in Gloucestershire, or sourced from like-minded local organic farms, and is delivered to the London shops each morning. The fruit and vegetables are grown in the market garden, the bread is baked in the bakery, and dairy products are produced in the creamery. As you wander around the shop you'll begin to fully appreciate the range and quality of the organic food on offer here and realise what a rare treat it is to be able to enjoy this authentic farm-to-table experience in central London. As well as a butcher and cheese and charcouterie counters – where you can sample the farm's own cheeses, such as Baywell, Adlestrop and Daylesford Cheddar – there's a deli section with fresh soups, pasta dishes and casseroles to take away and a good range of fresh eggs and groceries. A counter at the front of the shop offers sweet and savoury dishes to eat in or take away, or you can enjoy a more leisurely lunch in the upstairs café with its large communal tables and changing seasonal menu.

Other London branches:

208-212 Westbourne Grove, London W11 2RH
Selfridges Food Hall, 400 Oxford Street, London
W1A 1AB

While you're in the area...

This is a great area for foodies and you're just seconds away from the renowned chocolatier William Curley (page 72). The hot chocolate is legendary and, it goes without saying, that the truffles and patisserie are divine.

Franklins Farm Shop

155 Lordship Lane, London SE22 8HX
Tel: 020 8693 3992
Opening times: Mon–Sat 9am–6pm, Sun 10am–5pm
Train: East Dulwich

Although we all subscribe to the notion of eating seasonal produce, in reality it's very easy to waver off course and fill your basket with a round-the-world tour of fruit and vegetables. However, if you shop in Franklins, seasonal is pretty much all you'll get – aside from a few choice favourites – but you'll also get the best and the freshest locally sourced produce. This shop is definitely light on its food miles, as many of its gorgeous baskets and array of shelves are stocked with food from farms in nearby Kent. So there's no danger of your groceries festering on long-haul flights or sitting in chilled container lorries for days on end.

The cheese is predominantly English and includes the crumbly Crockhamdale and the vegetarian Norbury Blue, which is handmade on Norbury Park Farm. The drinks cabinet is eclectic and here you'll find apple juice, cider and a select choice of beer, ale and obscure English liqueurs. The mushrooms are wild, the eggs are organic and even the honey and jam are local, made in nearby Dulwich. Alright, so the onions and garlic might come from France but farmer, Laurent, personally brings his biodynamic crop over from Brittany and sells them from the back of his bicycle. But Franklins isn't just trading on a quirky 'everything's local' trait. The quality is superb and the range of goods in the shop merely highlights the fact that we have so many excellent food producers right on our doorstep. As if to prove the point, its sister venture, Franklins Restaurant, has been busy championing local ingredients for ten years with its no-nonsense seasonal menu.

While you're in the area...

Every other shop on this high street is a food-lover's treasure trove. William Rose (page 45) is an esteemed local butcher, just across the road from Franklins, while back towards the station you'll pass Green & Blue (page 160), The Cheeseblock (page 49), Moxon's fishmonger (page 100), SBMS organic grocers and East Dulwich Deli (page 78).

Highgate Village Fruiterers

3 Highgate High Street, London N6 5JR
Tel: 020 8340 0985
Opening times: Mon–Sun 8.30am–5.30pm,
Sun 10am–4pm
Tube: Highgate

The beautiful shop front has stepped crates of the freshest produce and a vast selection of blooms and bouquets, all creating a year-round spring aroma that will entice you inside. Here, you'll find more of the best quality seasonal and exotic fruit and vegetables, all of which have been carefully sourced by owner Michael. He gets up at some ungodly hour of the morning to select the best of what's on offer at Spitalfields Food Market. Unlike many buyers, Michael doesn't hurry through his list: he takes as long as it takes to find the absolute best of everything as his discerning Highgate clientele have come to expect the finest and freshest vegetables, fruit and flowers and nothing less will do.

Michael bought the shop in 1993 but he's been in the business all his working life, having followed in the footsteps of his father, who ran a successful greengrocer shop in Belsize Park. The motto was always 'quality, variety and good service' and it's easy to see that this shop has taken on the mantel. Sharon fruit, juicy fresh figs, whole beets, white onions, and beautiful Romanesco broccoli were just some of the produce on display when I visited and the steady flow of customers clearly demonstrates that people appreciate the superior quality of all this hand-chosen produce. Whilst supermarkets compete in terms of range and price, there's a lot to be said for a lifetime of knowledge and a keen eye for quality.

While you're in the area...

This road is a bit of a foodie treasure trove. If you fancy afternoon tea, step inside the delightful High Tea of Highgate. The Highgate Pantry makes a great lunch stop, while the Village Deli offers a good range of deli classics, along with homemade sandwiches and baguettes.

Michanicou Bros

2 Clarendon Road, London W11 3AA

Tel: 020 7727 5191

Opening times: Mon–Fri 9am–6.30pm,
Sat 9am–5.30pm

Tube: Holland Park

Chris and Andy are the brothers referred to in the shop name and they've been running this highly regarded Holland Park greengrocer since 1982. There's an infectious sense of energy as soon as you walk inside and it's incredible to think that these guys have been to Spitalfields Market and back to the shop before you or I have had our first cup of tea of the day. The early mornings, which are part and parcel of being a greengrocer (or baker or fishmonger), demonstrate the passion and commitment that they have for their produce and the produce here is second to none.

It's hard to believe that so many varieties of fresh fruit and vegetables can be crammed into such a compact space but there really is everything you could possibly need in here, including a good selection of organic produce. There are wild mushrooms, seasonal greens, vibrant salad leaves and seasonal specialities like Italian truffles. The shop offers a local daily delivery service, with customers phoning in their orders. It's all very community-focused and the locals are fiercely proud of this gem of a shop on their doorstep. But news of the quality and range of the produce on offer here has spread further afield and the brothers now supply a number of delis, butchers and other shops with their expertly sourced food. The green-striped awning is the only adornment to the shop. There are no superfluous furnishings or frills; there simply isn't the room. Every last inch of space is occupied by good-looking veggies.

While you're in the area...

Walk to Notting Hill Gate for catch of the day at James Knight of Mayfair (page 99). Or, take a leisurely stroll north towards Ladbroke Grove tube and you'll find Books for Cooks, a bookshop dedicated to foodies and a must-stop destination on any trip to W11. The Grocer on Elgin is just a minute from the reading matter and this is the place to go for top-end, homemade meals.

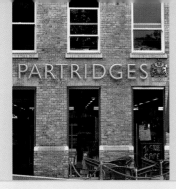

Partridges

2–5 Duke of York Square, London SW3 4LY
Tel: 020 7730 0651
Opening times: Mon–Sun 8am–10pm
Tube: Sloane Square

It seems something of an understatement to call this vast emporium of food and drink a grocery store and it could have been included in other chapters in the book. But its local feel and the fact it has remained a family-run business in the heart of cutthroat King's Road make the cosy, feel-good 'grocery' moniker fit like a glove. Richard Shepherd opened Partridges in 1972 and it still proudly trades with many of its original suppliers, as well as constantly sourcing new and unusual products to add to its vast line of household favourites and quality own-brand goods.

Partridges is located in Duke of York Square, much of which has been redeveloped over recent years to create a large, open public square and commercial space from a former military campus. The Partridges Food Market has been running every Saturday in the square outside the shop since 2005 and it's a local hub for quality, speciality producers, now attracting over 60 stalls on a regular basis. The shop itself is imposing and grand and inside it's decadently expansive, with its wide aisles and gloriously spacious displays encouraging leisurely browsing. The food has an upmarket feel but there's no pretentiousness here; it's all quality fare that would fit comfortably in any weekday larder, with a generous dose of treats and special occasion foods. Fruit and vegetables are stacked elegantly on an old vegetable barrow with further displays surrounding it and there's a wonderful beer and wine section with labels from around the world, including the British Gospel Green Cyder.

However, it's the deli counter that really makes Partridges a standout food destination. The vast four-sided counter takes up the entire centre of the shop and the choice of products is dizzying. There are rows of cheese, deli products, snacks, pies, quiches, freshly filled sandwiches and baguettes, as well as pastries, flans and mouth-watering cakes. The charcouterie puts other shops to shame and you'll find everything from biltong and Speck to Praga ham, Breseola, Mortadella and Bayonne ham here. And how about some fresh truffles to add a touch of decadence to your meal? If the choice is too great, you can always choose from prepared food like chicken Kiev, escalope, or lasagne, or sit down in the smart café area at the back of the shop. The trolleys by the door aren't just for show, people come to Partridges to do serious shopping and a basket simply won't cut the mustard. It's no surprise that this venerable shop is Grocers by Appointment to HM the Queen.

Other London branches:

17-21 Gloucester Road, London SW7 4PL

While you're in the area...

Don't leave the area without visiting Artisan du Chocolat (page 62) with its exquisite collection of truffles and bars. Keep walking until you get to Pimlico Road and step inside the wonderful world of Daylesford Organic (page 148), a feast for all the senses.

Yeomans

152 Regents Park Road, London NW1 8XN
Tel: 020 7722 4281
Opening times: Mon–Sat 8.30am–7pm, Sun
10am–5pm
Tube: Kentish Town

Nobody needs an excuse to travel to this gorgeous patch of London but if you're looking for one then use Yeomans. It's a beautiful, traditional greengrocer, which keeps things simple and uncluttered and concentrates on supplying quality fruit and vegetables to its well-heeled regulars. Fruit and flowers seem to be natural bedfellows and Yeomans has taken this on board by also selling a select range of flowers. These are displayed outside, next to tables of plump tomatoes and glossy oranges, providing a rainbow display of natural colours and an intoxicating scent for passers-by.

Phil has owned Yeomans for 25 years but it has been a greengrocer for over 120 years, making it one of the oldest shops in the area. His daily early morning trip to New Covent Garden Market sees him seeking out a full range of the best-quality fruit, vegetables and flowers. Everything is carefully arranged to its full advantage inside the shop, with lovely wooden display boxes, miniature chalkboards for prices by each variety and a neat stack of wicker shopping baskets. But it's the juice bar that really sets Yeomans apart. It seems perfectly natural to have a juice bar in a greengrocer and yet this is the first one I've seen. It's proven to be a popular spot for buying a fresh fruit smoothie or juice and Phil has created a menu including pear, watercress and spinach, and apple lemon and mint. A tiny garden sits behind the shop and it's an urban oasis with tables nestled amongst huge bamboos and ferns.

While you're in the area...

Cross the road to Richard Dare for a superlative selection of cookware, tableware and kitchen utensils. Melrose & Morgan on nearby Gloucester Avenue is a deli and grocery shop, but it also has a kitchen preparing delicious food to eat in or take away. Pop into Harry's Fine Food on Kentish Town Road before you get back on the tube.

WINE MERCHANTS

There's no better accompaniment to a nice meal than a bottle of fine wine, and London has a wine merchant to suit every taste and budget. In the pages that follow you'll be introduced to an Aladdin's Cave of specialist wine stores, each staffed by friendly and knowledgeable staff who will be only too happy to help match your chosen dish to a bottle of something delicious.

1 Berry Bros & Rudd
2 Bottle Apostle
3 Green & Blue
4 Jeroboams
5 Lea & Sandeman
6 Philglas & Swiggot
7 Planet of the Grapes
8 The Sampler
9 Theatre of Wine
10 Vagabond
11 Wimbledon Wine Cellar

Crouch End
Homsey
South Tottenham
Highgate
Finsbury Park
Stoke Newington
Kentish Town
Holloway
Belsize Park
Canonbury
Hackney
Chalk Farm
Kingsbury
Islington
Kensal Green
Ladbroke Grove
Archway
Regent's Park
Finsbury
Shoreditch
Bloomsbury
Shepherd's Bush
Paddington
West End
Soho
Moorgate
Holland Park
Mayfair
Hyde Park
Whitechapel
Kensington
Earl's Court
Knightsbridge
Strand
Southwark
Chiswick
Hammersmith
Westminster
Bermondsey
Rotherhithe
Isle of Dogs
Chelsea
Pimlico
Lambeth
Walworth
Barnes
Fulham
Deptford
Peckham
Putney
Battersea
Camberwell
Greenwich
Clapham
Brixton
Nunhead
Lewisham
Roehampton
Wandsworth
Balham
Dulwich
Catford
Tulse Hill

N

Berry Bros & Rudd

3 St. James's Street, London SW1A 1EG
Tel: 0800 280 2440
Opening times: Mon-Fri 10am-6pm,
Sat 10am-5pm, Sun closed
Tube: Green Park

In terms of history, longevity and quality, you'll find it hard to beat Berry Bros & Rudd. The original part of the large shop in the heart of St James dates back to 1698 when the Widow Bourne founded the business. Back in those days the shop was a grocers and the huge scales that were used to weigh tea and coffee (and latterly customers), still sit in the shop. The room is packed full of character and you could be mistaken for thinking that you've walked onto a period drama film set when you step inside. The dark wooden floor slopes sharply down to one side, while wood panelling, old whiskey barrels and antique furniture add to the ambience.

However, Berry Bros could never be accused of being stuck in the past. Various rooms lead off from the main space and the shop as a whole is a wonderfully clever combination of tradition and modernity. These rooms house the various collections of wine, Champagne and spirits and lush carpets, opulent dressers and chiller cabinets show off the bottles to their best advantage. Although the company is steeped in history, it was also the first wine merchant to launch its own website and its very aware of the need to embrace modern purchasing habits, with customers all over the world keen to buy from its vast range of wines and spirits.

As well as sourcing the finest and rarest wines from all over the world, Berry Bros offers en primeur services and a cellar plan, which could see you create your own enviable collection of wine over the years. The shop also holds regular tastings and fine wine dinners in some of the many rooms that form part of this grand old building.

While you're in the area...

Wander up to Piccadilly for some foodie treats in Fortnum & Mason (page 107), or cut down swish Jermyn Street for a grand selection of British and French cheeses in Paxton and Whitfield (page 57).

Bottle Apostle

95 Lauriston Road, London E9 7HJ
Tel: 020 8985 1549
Opening times: Mon closed, Tues-Fri 12pm-9pm,
Sat 10am-8pm, Sun 10am-6pm
Tube: Hackney Central or London Fields (mainline)

Bottle Apostle is one of a new wave of foodie ventures that has seen the fortunes of Hackney change over recent years. With its vibrant café scene and the glorious Victoria Park on its doorstep, this area of London is flourishing and its shops are seen as being part of the community. Bottle Apostle has quickly endeared itself into this foodie enclave by eschewing the traditional method of wine selection in favour of a more hands-on customer focused choice, which allows you to taste various wines in store before you commit to buying a whole bottle.

Tasting machines are becoming increasingly popular in wine merchants but the concept can only be successful when staff knowledge works in harmony with the freedom of choice that a wide tasting sample allows. At Bottle Apostle, the list of wines available to sample changes constantly, so there's always something new to try but it's the enthusiasm of the staff that really makes this a destination wine merchant. We've arrived in a time when a lot of people have a little knowledge about wine (I'm thinking of myself here) but we still hope for some direction and guidance when we wander into a shop. Here, people are encouraged to see the tastings as a way to experiment and perhaps stumble upon a new favourite. When I visited, I tried a Mallorcan red that would have normally passed way over my radar if it had simply been sitting on a shelf. And, if you're still not sure about what to serve at your next dinner party, the shop hosts a diverse range of tasting events ranging from cheese and wine evenings to a liquid book club.

While you're in the area...

Walk two doors along and you'll find the Ginger Pig (page 37). This branch is a deli as well as a butcher and it's stocked with the best groceries, meat and produce in the area. If you're here on a Saturday you have to wander around Broadway Market (page 132) for the atmosphere, as well as the food.

Green & Blue

38 Lordship Lane, London SE22 8HJ
Tel: 020 8693 9250
Opening times: Mon–Sat 9am–12am,
Sun 12pm–8pm
Train: East Dulwich

If you like your wine, you may already be familiar with this quirky wine shop with a truly original concept. Aside from stocking a fantastic range of wines from all manner of producers all over the world, Green & Blue positively encourages patrons to sit down and enjoy drinking their chosen bottle in the bar. This laid-back imbibing space is attached to the shop but it's in a separate room to ensure browsing and tasting can also be enjoyed independently. Incredibly, drink-in customers pay retail price for bottles of wine during the week, subject to a minimum spend, whilst at the weekend, there's a small corkage charge. This simple yet conceptually intriguing way to get up close and personal to wine in a truly convivial environment makes Green & Blue a stand-out shop.

However, a wine shop is only as good as its

wines and Green & Blue has proved itself with a wide range of carefully sourced bottles from small producers who just don't get the shelf space in most high street shops. The company specialises in organic, biodynamic wines and its philosophy of making wine buying a fun and interactive experience seems to be going down a storm in this trendy south-east London locale. Education is also a top priority and customers can take advantage of the range of tastings and School of Wine Courses that are regularly run in the shop.

The shop itself is a carefully considered blend of sleek, industrial-style display shelves, complemented by worn wooden floorboards. Think chic Parisian jazz cellar and you'll start to get the picture. Wines are grouped under easy labels, such as 'heavy', 'crisp' and 'spicy' and this makes for a great starting point for anyone who knows what they like but wants to try something a bit different. Once you've narrowed down your choice you can check out the detailed notes that accompany every bottle. How else would stumble upon such gems as Haridimos Hatzidakis, a venerated wine from a tiny producer on the Greek Island of Santorini? And, once you've chosen your wine and picked out a table in the bar, there's a wonderful menu of sharing platters, nibbles and hot food to help it go down.

While you're in the area...

Don't miss the East Dulwich Deli (page 78) just across the road, or take a stroll further along Lordship Lane for Moxon's (page 100), Franklin's Farm Shop (page 149) and William Rose (page 45).

Jeroboams

20 Davies Street, London W1K 3DT
Tel: 020 7499 1015
Opening times: Mon–Fri 9.30am–7pm,
Sat–Sun closed
Tube: Bond Street

Although the Jeroboams name is instantly associated with fine wine, the company actually began life as a cheesemonger, with the first shop opening in South Kensington in 1985. Since then the twin pleasures of wine and cheese have helped this chain of shops, which are linked by name but vary vastly in character, to become one of the greats in the London food world. Whilst the shop in Holland Park is still primarily a cheesemonger (and a fine one at that) and some other branches do stock cheese and high-end grocery items alongside their prestigious wine selections, most of the central London shops are now solely dedicated to the grape.

The Mayfair shop is as traditional a wine merchant as you'd expect to find in this wealthy London locale, just south of Oxford Street. If you make your escape from the super-sized fashion stores and crowds of shoppers, you'll be rewarded with the chance to regain your breath and your sanity in this quiet little wine lover's enclave. Inside the shop, bottles stand to attention like soldiers on parade and there's a pleasing minimalism to the whole display, which allows you to focus on the important business of choosing a wine. And if you need help, the unassuming advice of the ultra knowledgeable staff will gently steer you towards the right wine. Why fumble about cluelessly in a supermarket when you can have expertise on tap in a shop like this? Although there's plenty here for the bulkier wallet, there's also a great deal of choice for everyday wines and more moderate means. When I visited, the wine of the moment was a beautiful South African Shiraz (2006 Tahbilk). For a few pounds over a tenner, it was certainly worth every penny.

Other London branches:

50-52 Elizabeth Street, London SW1W 9PB

6 Pont Street, London SW1X 9EL

29 Heath Street, London NW3 6TR

96 Holland Park Avenue, London W11 3RB

56 Walton Street, London SW3 1RB

13 Elgin Crescent, London W11 2JA

1 St John's Wood High Street, London NW8 7NG

3 Greek Street, London W1D 4NX (Milroy's of Soho)

While you're in the area...

Step back in history when you walk into Allen's of Mayfair (page 30) or stop for a quality coffee and sandwich in The Mount Street Deli.

Lea & Sandeman

170 Fulham Road, London SW10 9PR
Tel: 020 7244 0522
Opening hours: Mon–Sat 10am–8pm,
Sun closed
Tube: South Kensington

The smart grey exterior of this original Lea & Sandeman store is a pretty good indication of what you'll discover inside. The shop is well laid-out, easy to navigate and packed to the rafters with wine. The displays run floor to ceiling and crates act as display units, showing off the bottles au naturel. There's an obvious respect for and love of good wine in here as, when the space runs out on the shelves, crates are neatly lined up on the wooden floors. It's as if every bottle on the their books should be given its cameo and the buying public given every opportunity to sample this range of carefully collected classics.

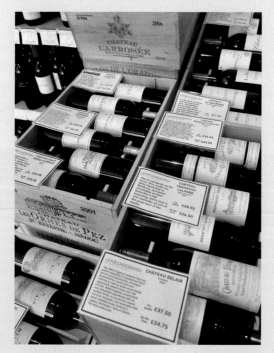

The emphasis here (and at the other three Lea & Sandeman branches) is to source wine that you want to keep drinking, not just wines with fancy labels from big name producers. Patrick Sandeman and Charles Lea source their wines directly from the producers and always have done, thus cutting out the middle man and ensuring that everything they sell has earned its right to be displayed. Customers trust their buying acumen and appreciate this attention to detail, which has resulted in a full range of wines from traditional producers as well as more innovative labels. Lea & Sandeman specialises in French and Italian wines and there's a good range of bottles for every budget, so there's no need to wander past if your wallet is a little light. The staff are more than happy to impart their knowledge and search out something new and exciting for your dinner table and nothing is too much trouble. Shops like this offer the best way to widen your wine knowledge and this is one of the best in town.

Other London branches:

211 Kensington Church Street, London W8 7LX
51 High Street, London SW13 9LN
167 Chiswick High Road, London W4 2DR

While you're in the area...

Indulge your sweet tooth with some stunning chocolate from Demarquette (page 65), which is seconds away. Walk an equal distance in the other direction and you'll be spoilt for choice in Luigi's Italian deli (page 82).

BIN ENDS

Philglas & Swiggot

21 Northcote Road, London SW11 1NG
Tel: 020 7924 4494
Opening times: Mon-Fri 11am-7pm, Sat 10am-6pm,
Sun 12pm-5pm
Train: Clapham Junction

If a shop's name were the exclusive criteria for greatness then Philglas & Swiggot would be top of the list every time. Luckily, it doesn't need to rely on its delightfully quirky name: the wines and the customer service at this independent merchant ensure its list of awards and accolades keeps getting longer every year.

The Northcote Road shop is wonderfully laid-back and welcoming. Not that it shouldn't be; it's just that people sometimes feel intimidated about the prospect of buying their grape juice from anywhere but a supermarket shelf. The reassurance of a recognisable label or a cut-price deal lures us in like a fishhook. But a good wine merchant can introduce you to a whole world of new producers, grapes, and styles of wine that simply aren't available in the local superstore. The staff in Philglas & Swiggot are only too happy to advise and recommend and there's something truly uplifting about walking out of a shop with a purchase that has been chosen specially for you, rather than one that has landed in your basket through habit or harassment.

This sense of openness and enthusiasm, combined with a genuine disappointment with the existing anodyne alcohol shopping experience is what initially persuaded owners Mike and Karen Rogers to open their first shop. They obviously weren't alone in their desire for a friendly, local wine merchant that offered exceptional choice and a bit of hand holding for wine newbies: they now have two more shops in London and a fiercely loyal clientele. They stock wine from all over the world but make it a priority to seek out the best that each region has to offer. That doesn't necessarily mean the priciest and, although there are a fair few bottles that empty the average wallet, the emphasis really is on quality and there are plenty of options for every budget.

Other London branches

22 New Quebec Street, London W1H 7SB
64 Hill Rise, Richmond, Surrey TW10 6UB

While you're in the area...

Wine and cheese are natural partners so once you've sorted out the alcohol, pop across the road to Hamish Johnston (page 52) for the perfect cheese pairing.

Planet of the Grapes

9 New Oxford Street, London WC1A 1BA
Tel: 020 7405 4912
Opening times: Mon 10am–6pm, Tues–Fri
10am–7pm, Sat–Sun Closed
Tube: Holborn

I'm not a sci-fi fan so the play on words for this independent wine merchant didn't really grab me. However, whatever your thoughts on paronomasia (that's a pun to you and me), you'll be seriously impressed once you walk inside, and the name is actually rather fitting. The densely packed wooden shelves and quirky wine case display units reach up to the ceiling and every inch of space is economically utilised. Detailed handwritten notes accompany every bottle. With a constantly evolving range to choose from, a lot of time and effort has obviously been spent in ensuring that useful pointers are given for new or unusual wines.

And new and unusual is exactly what Planet of the Grapes prides itself on sourcing. Whilst other establishments might turn their noses up at wines from emerging producers or as yet established regions or grape varieties, you'll find everything here, as long as it passes the taste test with the buyers. Customers here trust the palates and noses of the staff and, in return, they get high quality wines at reasonable prices. Of course, price is always relative to your means but there's plenty in every price range here and there is such a wide range of wines to try that you need to trust the judgement of the staff and push your wine drinking boundaries. Regular tasting evenings are held in the tasting cellar to introduce people to some of the most exciting wine producers of the moment and these are always laid-back and unpretentious events.

Other London branches:

9/10 Bulls Head Passage, London, EC3V 1LU

While you're in the area...

You're literally 30 seconds away from one of my favourite cafes. Wild & Wood is a gorgeously appointed little coffee shop serving Monmouth Coffee and Villandry pastries. With its wood panelling and cosy corners it's a haven from the big, bad world. A quick stretch of the legs along Tottenham Court Road will bring you to Peyton & Byrne for a selection of baked treats to take home.

The Sampler

266 Upper Street, London N1 2UQ
Tel: 020 7226 9500
Opening times: Mon–Sat 11.30am–9pm,
Sun 11.30am–7pm
Tube: Highbury & Islington or Angel

This smart wine merchant on the perpetually popular Upper Street aims to bring wine to a larger audience and it seems to have pulled it off. A simple but effective concept has changed the way that locals can choose and buy their wine, ensuring that they walk out of the door with a bottle they'll enjoy, rather than making a snap decision based on the label or the price tag. At any one time, there are 80 wines to sample and the price of a single tasting is directly proportionate to the retail price of the bottle. The Sampler was the first wine merchant in the country to introduce sampling machines. These clever devices restrict oxygen from the bottles, so the wine stays as fresh as a daisy for a number of weeks. The wines are constantly switched and owners, Dawn and Jamie, aim to offer every single wine in the shop as a sampler at some point and with some 1,500 different wines on offer, that's no mean feat. Whenever you visit you'll find a good selection of everyday wines, as well as some of the world's finest in the 'Icon Machine'.

This interactive wine buying experience is a great way to introduce people to exciting new wines and it also allows customers to try some prohibitively expensive bottles that they might never have the opportunity to sample otherwise. A bottle of Jaboulet Thalabert Crozes Hermitage 1978 would set you back well over £100 but it was a sampler when I popped in and could be sipped and savoured for a fraction of the price. The shop is well laid-out and cheerily laid back, which fittingly works with the original idea to make wine-buying fun and the wines approachable. Although the staff are always on hand to help out, there's definitely a sense of buying power here. You might not have a sommelier's palate but you are following the judgement of your own taste buds, rather than someone else's.

Other London branches:

35 Thurloe Place, London SW7 2HJ

While you're in the area...

Cross the road to Euphorium (page 19) for some of the best bread in town or take a side step along Camden Passage for Paul A. Young's gorgeous chocolate shop (page 68). The lovely little Italian deli, Olga Stores (page 83) is just a ten-minute walk away on Penton Street.

Theatre of Wine

75 Trafalgar Road, London SE10 9TS
Tel: 020 8858 6363
Opening times: Mon–Sat 10am–9pm,
Sun 12pm–6pm
Train: Maze Hill

It comes as no great surprise that owner Daniel is from a theatrical background. Aside from the name of the shop, the interior pays exquisite but tasteful homage to the stage. Plush drapes frame the constantly changing window display and ornate chairs surround a massive table that is the centrepiece of the room. The business has expanded rapidly since the shop was first opened in 2002, so much so that there's now a second shop in Tufnell Park. However, although the Greenwich branch certainly filled a gaping hole in the market at the time of opening, its success really comes down to dedication and customer service.

Daniel firmly believes that tasting is one of the most important aspects of the business. This is how new wines are introduced, how relationships are formed and how the loyal customer base is expanded. Having been to a number of tasting events here myself, I can see exactly what he means. The evenings are informal and the emphasis is always about encouraging people to experiment without taking them completely out of their comfort zone. There's a story behind every bottle and a great deal of artisan bread, ham and cheese to soak up the alcohol.

Theatre of Wine is unusual in that it doesn't specialise in any country, region or production method, although they do tend to focus on smaller, independent producers. The range of wines in the shop is a result of constant travelling, tasting and careful choosing. It's an eclectic selection that is updated and added to constantly, with preference being given to local grape varieties, distinctive flavours and wines with a tale to tell.

Other London branches:

124 Junction Road, London N19 5LB

While you're in the area...

It would be a crying shame not to pop into The Old Brewery while you're in Greenwich. It's just a 5-minute walk down the road in the Old Royal Naval College and here you can enjoy one of the many beers created by the Meantime Brewing Company, including Pale Ale, Wheat Beer and Meantime Chocolate. Another short walk will bring you to the wonderful Rhodes Bakery (page 27) and Greenwich Market.

Vagabond

18-22 Vanston Place, London SW6 1AX
Tel: 020 7381 1717
Opening hours: Mon-Fri 12pm-9pm,
Sat 11am-9pm, Sun 11am-6pm
Tube: Fulham Broadway

Vagabond only opened in 2010 but it has already made a big impression on the wine buying habits of its Fulham clientele. The huge space is light, bright and so conducive to sticking around and sampling what's on offer that it's lucky you can do exactly that. The ethos behind the shop is to make wine simple and more accessible and the concept here replicates this to the letter. There are roughly 100 wines in the shop and although the range on offer here is far fewer than in other wine merchants, each and every bottle has been given serious consideration before it's allowed its hallowed space on the shelf.

The owners wanted to cut through the confusion and offer a select range of wines that they have tasted, tested, know intimately and would happily recommend to customers. The difference here is that all these wines can be tasted before you commit to buying a bottle. Tasting cabinets are spread around the shop and you can opt for a small taster or a whole glass, which you are welcome to enjoy at the large dining table, or in one of the comfy sofas. More recently, the shop has introduced a small food menu so you really can relax and take your time. The stock is constantly updated so that regulars have the opportunity to try a range of new wines every month and each bottle has detailed tasting notes, as well as key information about the wine, region, food pairing and style. I tried a Juan Gil Monastrell 2009 and the notes were spot on: you can even take the tasting cards with you to use as a prompt for your next visit.

Wines are grouped by style to make it easy to navigate your way towards new wines in the style you know you like and regular tasting evenings also help to introduce customers to wines they might not normally consider. Personally, I'd use any excuse to make a bee-line for this gorgeous concept wine merchant that positively encourages lingering.

While you're in the area...

Union Market (page 116) is next to Fulham Broadway tube station and this is one-stop food shop with a bakery section, butcher, cheese and fish counters, a grocers and great options for both take out and eat-in food.

Wimbledon Wine Cellar

4 The Boulevard, Imperial Wharf, London SW6 2UB
Tel: 020 7736 2191
Opening hours: Mon–Sat 10am–9pm, Sun 11am–6pm
Tube: Imperial Wharf

If you have never seen a grand piano in the centre of a wine merchant before then you should definitely pay Wimbledon Wine Cellar a visit. This gloriously frivolous use of space can only be appreciated once you've stepped inside the vast shop: from the wines themselves to the carefully designed and defined areas for tasting, relaxing and dining, every detail has been carefully considered to add to the ambience and grandeur of this destination shop which opened in 2005. I say destination as, although it's only a minute's walk from a zone 2 tube station, this part of town is a little off the beaten track in terms of foodie neighbours. But whatever you do, please don't let that put you off.

You could easily while away a whole afternoon here, working your way along the shelves that are home to a staggering 1,000 bottles of wine at any time. In fact, there's so much to discover and absorb that a cosy seating area with armchairs lets you take the weight off your feet while you mull over your choices, or chat with the staff about your requirements. As the shop is independent the staff have complete control over the wines that are stocked, and although it is particularly well known for its ranges of Italian, Burgundy and Bordeaux wines, there's plenty of choice from all over the world, including a growing selection of interesting new world wines, particularly from South America. The list is constantly evolving, changing and growing and customers are encouraged to engage in the exciting discovery of new producers and regions. Regular tasting dinners also introduce people to new wines and producers are encouraged to come and discuss their wine. The laid-back dinners are held around the massive dining table and are all about pairing fine wine with good food in a unique environment.

Other London branches

84 Chiswick High Road, London W4 1SY
1 Gladstone Road, London SW19 1QU

While you're in the area...

Randall's butcher (page 42) is a ten-minute walk away on Wandsworth Bridge Road and is well worth the short hike. There's a wonderful selection of free range and organic meat, as well as stuffed and prepped cuts that are ready to cook.

WORLD FOOD

London is home to people of many ethnicities with a diverse range of communities originating from every corner of the globe, and this is reflected in the wide variety of world food stores in the capital. From Greek, Spanish and Moroccan to Japanese, Thai and Chinese, every taste and cuisine is catered for. It really is worth a trip to visit the stores listed here, not only for the wonderful and unusual produce available, but also for the experience of stepping into another world and absorbing a little bit of what that country has to offer.

1 Athenian Grocery
2 Green Valley
3 Japan Centre
4 Le Maroc
5 Loon Fung
6 R. Garcia & Sons
7 Taj Stores
8 Talad Thai
9 Turkish Food Centre

Crouch End

Homsey

South
Tottenham

Highgate

Finsbury
Park

Stoke
Newington

Kentish Town

Holloway

Belsize Park

Canonbury

Hackney

Chalk
Farm

Kingsbury

Islington

Harlesden

Regent's
Park

Finsbury

Shoreditch

Kensal
Green

Ladbroke
Grove

Archway

Bloomsbury

Moorgate

4

Shepherd's
Bush

Paddington

West End

7

Holland
Park

6

Soho

Whitechapel

Mayfair

1

2

3 5

Hyde Park

Strand

Kensington

Southwark

Westminster

Bermondsey

Rotherhithe

Chiswick

Hammersmith

Earl's Court

Knightsbridge

Lambeth

Isle of
Dogs

Chelsea

Pimlico

Walworth

Barnes

Fulham

Battersea

Camberwell

Peckham

Deptford

Greenwich

8

Putney

Clapham

Nunhead

Lewisham

Roehampton

Wandsworth

Brixton

Dulwich

N

Balham

Catford

Tulse Hill

Athenian Grocery

16a Moscow Road, London W2 4BT
Tel: 020 7229 6280
Opening hours: Mon–Sat 8.30am–7pm,
Sun 9.30am–1pm
Tube: Bayswater

This tidy corner shop is the favoured destination for members of the Greek and Greek Cypriot communities in London and further afield. It's very traditional in style, with striped awnings and boxes of fresh produce stacked outside and an interior crammed with everyday and more unusual Greek ingredients. The utilitarian

décor ensures that no space is left empty and the large counter takes centre stage. Here you'll find cheese and a huge selection of delicious olives, stuffed vine leaves and other loose deli treats. There's wonderful baklava, dips, fresh loaves, dried fruit, canned meat and fish, cakes, biscuits, olive oil and a good range of ready-to-eat snacks. The staff are only too happy to enlighten Greek food first-timers about the provenance of everything stocked in the shop and offer advice on how to prepare and eat the wonderful array of choice produce and products.

The quality here makes it well worth a visit, even if you're just looking for a selection of nibbles or a really good wedge of feta or halloumi cheese. It's also a great place to stop by for the makings of a picnic in nearby Hyde Park. They've got everything you need for an al fresco Mediterranean feast.

While you're in the area...

Check out Planet Organic in Westbourne Grove (page 113) for a huge range of natural foods. It's like a feel-good supermarket in the centre of London. Alternatively, head south to Notting Hill Gate and soak up the atmosphere while you take advantage of the fantastic food shopping. Try James Knight of Mayfair (page 99), Chegworth Farm Shop (page 147) and Clarke's (page 15) for starters.

SORRY
BUT WE DO
NOT
ACCEPT
CREDIT CARDS

Green Valley

36-37 Upper Berkeley Street, London W1H 5QF
Tel: 020 7402 7385
Opening times: Mon–Sun 8am–12am
Tube: Marble Arch

Even in an area of London that is well known for its plethora of Middle Eastern shops, cafes and restaurants, Green Valley still stands out. This double fronted food store with its welcoming green awnings is a destination Lebanese supermarket and with good reason. It manages to combine workaday staples with luxury foodstuffs in its packed interior. At any given time there are people stocking up with a week's worth of groceries, alongside those who have popped in for a mid-afternoon halva pick-me-up. The shop is a treasure trove of treats from a bounteous country that stretches along the Mediterranean Sea.

The sumptuous pyramids of sweet delights are simply breathtaking and will challenge even the sweetest tooth. Once you've paused to admire these, you can move on to the huge barrels of olives, the lengthy cheese and meat counter and the mounds of freshly prepared snacks, warm and ready to eat. A substantial freezer offers plenty of options for take-home meals, whilst the selection of dates, dried fruit and nuts brings a whole new meaning to the word 'snack'. Intricately stacked shelves offer every possible variety of dried peas, beans, spices, cartons, cans and oil that you could wish for. There's also a fresh produce aisle, where Lebanese vegetables are neatly arranged next to Western favourites. The whole shop is scented with a deliciously subtle aroma of spices and the browsing and choosing experience is a pleasure, especially when rounded off with a couple of pieces of gooey, sweet baklava.

While you're in the area...

If there's any space left in your shopping bags, it's not too far to Selfridges Food Hall (page 115) on Oxford Street. It's a completely different vibe but just as rewarding for the palate. You're also very close to being spoilt for choice on Marylebone High Street...just make sure your diary is empty and your wallet is full.

Japan Centre

14-16 Regent Street, London SW1Y 4PH
Tel: 020 3405 1246
Opening times: Mon–Sat 10am–9pm,
Sun 11am–7pm
Tube: Piccadilly Circus

This shop in the heart of Piccadilly is deceptively large and just when you think you've seen it all, more aisles of fresh food, groceries and cooking ingredients spread out before you. It's all here: there's freshly baked bread and rolls in the bakery section at the front of the shop, including baked curry bread, anpan, edamame and sesame bread, and butter rolls. Opposite this you'll find a food bar offering delicious meals, plus snacks like dumplings and gyoza, which you can take away or eat in at one of the communal dining tables.

Moving on there's a huge fridge with an endless array of freshly prepared sushi rolls, inari and sashimi, which is constantly refreshed. Another chilled section offers a multitude of tofu incarnations and yet another is laden down with sake and soft drinks. A further range of sakes sits on an aisle opposite, clearly marked out as bottles to be imbibed warm. A large meat and fish counter offers yet another opportunity to try some of the handmade sushi and sashimi and this leads on to the large grocery section. I love all the packets of dried noodles and snacks in brightly coloured packaging, the miso paste, the huge sacks of rice and the endless variety of green and jasmine tea. Everything is clearly labelled and priced in English, as well as Japanese, and the staff are incredibly helpful and friendly. It's a great place to shop for ingredients, or stop for some authentic Japanese fast food.

While you're in the area...

You're just a few minutes' walk away from Paxton & Whitfield (page 57) with its incredible selection of cheese. Walk north and you'll find yourself in Soho where Lina Stores (page 81) sells all things Italian, including homemade pasta and sauces.

Le Maroc

94 Golbourne Road, London W10 5PS
Tel: 020 8968 9783
Opening hours: Mon–Sat 9am–8pm, Sun closed
Tube: Ladbroke Grove or Westbourne Park

This is a little corner of Morocco in the heart of London. The long, narrow shop alerts your senses to the sights, sounds and smells of the North African country. The Halal butcher counter is at the front of the shop and there's a wide selection of joints and cuts of meat, as well as prepared kofte and sausages. On the shelves opposite there are endless varieties of dates and apricots, nuts, vine leaves, olive oil, tinned fish, harissa, fava beans, cereals and snacks.

Walk through to the other end of the shop and you'll find chilled drinks, yogurt, salami and cold meats, as well as huge barrels of olives, tubs of preserved lemons, tea, coffee and Turkish delight. Customers browse, shop and chat and there's a real sense of community here, with the shop providing so much more than mere provisions. It's a hub of Moroccan culture, as well as food, but it also offers a great introduction to the cuisine and ingredients of the region for anyone embarking on a North African cooking extravaganza. And, if there's anything you need to know, the staff are always ready to help out and only too happy to advise on ingredients and cooking tips.

While you're in the area...

Check out Golbourne Fisheries (page 97) for a huge selection of fresh fish and seafood. The Grain Shop on Portobello Road attracts bread lovers from all over town, while R. Garcia & Sons (page 182) is the place to go for Spanish cured meats, cheeses and groceries. When you're ready for a coffee break, head to Golbourne Deli or Coffee Plant.

Loon Fung

42-44 Gerrard Street, London W1D 5QG
Tel: 020 7437 7332
Opening times: Mon-Sun 10am–9.30pm
Tube: Leicester Square

Chinatown is neatly tucked between Soho, Covent Garden and Piccadilly. Gerrard Street is a hub of Chinese restaurants and shops with a level of kinetic energy that's pretty hard to match anywhere else in the city and Loon Fung is in the heart of it. The double frontage of this pan-Asian supermarket is completely taken over by boxes of fresh fruit and vegetables. There's more produce inside with equal measure of everyday ingredients and more unusual Asian specialities like eddo, yellow plum, mooli, sugar cane and garlic sprouts.

Continue your shopping trip and you'll discover aisles of groceries with everything from Chinese sausages to green tea. There's a whole aisle of spices and dried herbs and a large section at the back of the shop dedicated to cooking utensils and equipment at very reasonable prices. You can pick up wooden steamers for the price of a cup of tea and there are various Sake sets, tea sets and woks. There are noodles of every size, variety and description and the rice shelves offer the same level of choice. Walk through to the next room and it's back to fresh food, with a long butcher counter and a chilled cabinet full of fish and tofu. It's perennially busy in here, which is always a good indication of the loyalty of local shoppers and its handy location makes it as viable to visit for a packet of noodles as for the ingredients for a sumptuous dinner party.

Other London branches:

111 Brantwood Road, London N17 0DX
Factory Road, London E16 2EJ

While you're in the area...

Chinatown backs onto Soho so make the most of its proximity and check out Lina Stores (page 81) and i Camisa & Son (page 80), two high-quality delis in the midst of the hedonism of Soho.

R. Garcia & Sons

246-250 Portobello Road, London W11 1LL
Tel: 020 7221 6119
Opening hours: Mon–Sun 10am–6pm
Tube: Ladbroke Grove

I stumbled on Garcia's purely by accident but it became an instant favourite. From the Spanish music playing through the speakers to the constant bustle of people on a shopping – rather than a mere browsing – mission, this is a utilitarian shop with an unsurpassed selection of Spanish foods. Brothers Tony and Rafael Garcia run the business, which was founded by their grandfather back in 1957. Pride and passion in the shop emanate from every shelf: the interior is spotless, staff are omnipresent but unobtrusive and the shelves are packed tightly and neatly.

The shop has a large grocery section with aisles of jars, packets, tins and boxes and everything from artichoke hearts, green peppercorns and Padron peppers to Amaretti, cakes, bread, flour and tea. There's a very good wine section, and a large deli counter that runs along the back of the shop. Here, knife-wielding staff wait to slice delicate slivers from whole hams and other charcouterie such as Lomo, Chorizo and Pancetta. Next to this, there are tubs of olives, sun-dried tomatoes, giant caper berries, cheeses, Catalan herb parcels and other choice deli delights. The shop also sells cooking dishes, coffee pots and utensils. Next door, there's a popular café serving tapas and light bites but get there early on the weekend, the place is usually packed.

While you're in the area...

You're very close to the Mr Christian's on Elgin Crescent and this fine shop offers a great range of deli products and made-to-order sandwiches. Stop for a coffee at Coffee Plant or head back onto Golbourne Road and you can discover the flavours of Morocco in Le Maroc (page 180).

Taj Stores

112 Brick Lane, London E1 6RL
Tel: 020 7377 0061
Opening times: Mon–Sun 9am–9pm
Tube: Liverpool Street, Aldgate East

Taj Stores has been selling its expansive range of groceries since 1936 and this gem of a shop remains one of the best places in London to source quality Asian ingredients. However, it also stocks a substantial range of food from all over the world and it's a truly international affair. I could spend hours just browsing the endless shelves of spices, which offer an incredible range at pretty incredible prices. Once you've seen how much you can get for your money here, you'll never buy one of those miniscule spice jars from the supermarket again. There are literally hundreds of bags, boxes and tubs of dried spices, herbs and pulses, huge cans of cooking oil, and endless sacks of rice stacked like flood water defences. The freezers are packed full of frozen fish blocks, tiny shrimps, massive prawns and whole fish that would require something more robust than a carrier bag to get them home.

The service too, makes this shop a pleasure to return to, as nothing is too much trouble. From chopping meat to locating ingredients, the staff are more than happy to help and advise, although the layout of the shop makes searching the endless aisles fairly straightforward. There's even a section for cooking utensils, with everything from woks to kaharis, making this a genuine one-stop shop for Asian cuisine. It's no great surprise that celebrity chefs and food writers make a beeline for this shop.

While you're in the area...

Walk north along Brick Lane and you'll arrive at Beigel Bake (no. 159), one of the best bakeries in the area. This is the place to go for a salt beef sandwich and, naturally, bagels. If you happen to be in the area on a Sunday then stay on Brick Lane for Upmarket at The Old Truman Brewery (page 129). Otherwise, you can head south to Spitalfields with its array of quality food shops. Check out Androuet (page 48), Montezuma's (page 67) and A. Gold (page 144).

Talad Thai

326 Upper Richmond Road, London SW15 6TL
Tel: 020 8789 8084
Opening hours: Mon–Sat 9am–8pm, Sun 10am–8pm
Tube: East Putney (or Putney Rail mainline)

Talad Thai first opened its doors in 1990 with the aim of bringing Thai food and ingredient knowledge to Londoners. Since then, interest in this southeast Asian cuisine has sky rocketed as the punchy flavours and fast prep times have slotted in comfortably to the London food scene and people have become more acquainted with the dishes and flavours of the country. Sa-ard and Thanaporn Kriangsak own and run the successful supermarket, whilst next door, there's a restaurant of the same name, making this corner of Putney a real destination for Thais looking for a taste of home, and foodies with Thai-focused taste buds.

Inside, the couple have made careful use of every inch of space and you'll make slow progress as you stop every second step to pick something else off the shelves. Classic Thai ingredients are in abundance including the now well-known kaffir lime leaves and the durian fruit, which is as famous for its pungent smell as its delicious flavour. Despite the shop name, there's a range of ingredients and produce from all over Asia here and you'll find a good selection of Chinese and Japanese cooking ingredients and herbs and a wide range of imported fruit and vegetables from all over the region. If you're just dipping your toe into Thai cuisine, this is the ideal shop to visit and you'll get plenty of help and advice from the staff. There's even cooking utensils and cookbooks so you really don't need to go anywhere else.

While you're in the area...

Walk down to the other end of Upper Richmond Road and you can swap Thai food for Italian. Valentina is an impressive deli and restaurant with all the ingredients could hope to find for an authentic Italian feast. Alternatively, a quick tube ride will take you to Fulham Broadway and here you can visit the incredible Union Market (page 116) and nearby Vagabond Wines (page 171).

TIN PRODUCTS

Turkish Food Centre

89 Ridley Road, London E8 2NP
Tel: 020 7254 6754
Opening times: Mon–Sat 8am–9pm,
Sun 8.30am–7.30pm
Tube: Dalston Kingsland

This is the original branch of the business that now has 14 supermarkets in the greater London area. The lengthy opening hours and sheer range of stock is testament to its success but it also shows the keen interest in Turkish ingredients and cuisine, which has spread far beyond the Turkish community. However, despite the name, this chain of shops stocks ingredients from all over the Mediterranean, having expanded and diversified over the years. All the branches are supermarket size and this means that people really do travel here to do their weekly shop. In turn the shop obliges by supplying a great range of products and there's choice in all areas.

The fresh produce aisle is laden down with a huge selection of constantly changing seasonal fruit and vegetables and it's a welcome treat to see a shop of this size stocking what's available in season. In the grocery section, as expected, there are rows of olives oils, a good range of dried goods such as beans and pulses, nuts, seeds and rice, and plenty of other storecupboard essentials. There's a lengthy halal butcher counter with plump chickens, lamb joints, and goat meat. An in-store bakery (there's one in every supermarket) ensures a constant supply of fresh bread, pastries and treats such as Baklava, and there's a fantastic cheese and deli counter with classic cheeses from across the Mediterranean region.

Other London branches:

647-661 High Road, London E11 4RD
363 Fore Street, London N9 0NR

163-165 Bromley Road, London SE6 2NZ
227-229 Lewisham High Street, London SE13 6LY
542-544 Lordship Lane, London N22 5BY
678-682 Tottenham High Road, London N17

While you're in the area...

If you happen to be out and about on a Saturday don't miss nearby Broadway Market (page 132), one of the best in London and it's an easy 20-minute walk away. Continue another ten minutes or so and you'll reach Lauriston Road, where Bottle Apostle (page 159) and Ginger Pig (page 37) tempt shoppers inside with their gorgeous selections of fine wine and quality meat.

ADDRESSES

Bakeries

Breadstall
60 Northcote Road SW11 1PA

Clarke's
122 Kensington Church Street
W8 4BH

De Gustibus
53-55 Carter Lane EC4V 5AE

Euphorium
202 Upper Street N1 1RQ

Exeter Street Bakery
1b Argyll Road W8 7DB

Gail's
64 Hampstead High Street NW3 1QH

Konditor & Cook
22 Cornwall Road SE1 8TW

The Old Post Office Bakery
76 Landor Road SW9 9PH

Poilâne
46 Elizabeth Street SW1W 9PA

Paul Rhodes Bakery
37 King William Walk SE10 9HU

Butchers

Allens of Mayfair
117 Mount Street W1K 3LA

C. Lidgate
110 Holland Park Avenue W11 4UA

Dove & Son
71 Northcote Road SW11 6PJ

Drings
22 Royal Hill SE10 8RT

Frank Godfrey
7 Highbury Park N5 1QL

The Ginger Pig
8-10 Moxon Street W1U 4EW

M. Moen & Sons
24 The Pavement SW4 0JA

Porterford
72 Watling Street EC4M 9BJ

Randalls
113 Wandsworth Bridge Road
SW6 2TE

William Rose
126 Lordship Lane SE22 8HD

Cheesemongers

Androuet
107b Commercial Street E1 6BG

The Cheese Block
69 Lordship Lane SE22 8EP

The Cheeseboard
26 Royal Hill SE10 8RT

Hamish Johnston
48 Northcote Road SW11 1PA

La Fromagerie
30 Highbury Park N5 2AA

Neal's Yard Dairy
17 Shorts Gardens WC2H 9AT

Paxton & Whitfield
93 Jermyn Street SW1Y 6JE

Rippon Cheese Stores
26 Upper Tachbrook Street
SW1V 1SW

Chocolatiers

Artisan du Chocolat
89 Lower Sloane Street SW1W 8DA

Charbonnel et Walker
One The Royal Arcade, 28 Old Bond
Street W1S 4BT

Demarquette
285 Fulham Road SW10 9PZ

Hotel Chocolat
163 Kensington High Street W8 6SU

Montezuma's
51 Brushfield Street E1 6AA

Paul A. Young
33 Camden Passage N1 8EA

Rococo Chocolates
5 Motcomb Street SW1X 8JU

Theobroma Cacao
43 Turnham Green Terrace W4 1RG

William Curley
198 Ebury Street SW1W 8UN

Delicatessens

Alimentari
342 Kilburn Lane W9 3EF

Brindisa
Stoney Street, Borough Market
SE1 9AF

East Dulwich Deli
15–17 Lordship Lane SE22 8EW

I Camisa & Son
61 Old Compton Street W1D 6HS

Lina Stores
18 Brewer Street W1F 0SH

Luigi's
349 Fulham Road SW10 9TW

Olga Stores
30 Penton Street N1 9PS

Ottolenghi
287 Upper Street N1 2TZ

Panzer's
13–19 Circus Road NW8 6PB

Trinity Stores
5 & 6 Balham Station Road
SW12 9SG

Fishmongers

Brown's
37–39 Charlbert Street NW8 6JN

The Chelsea Fishmonger
10 Cale Street SW3 3QU

**Covent Garden
Fishmongers**
37 Turnham Green Terrace W4 1RG

FishWorks
89 Marylebone High Street W1U 4QW

Golborne Fisheries
77 Golborne Road W10 5NL

James Knight of Mayfair
67 Notting Hill Gate W11 3JS

Moxon's
149 Lordship Lane SE22 8HX

Steve Hatt
88–90 Essex Road N1 8LU

Food Halls and Emporiums

Food Hall
374–378 Old Street EC1V 9LT

Fortnum & Mason
181 Piccadilly W1A 1ER

Greensmiths
27 Lower Marsh SE1 7RG

Harrods
87–135 Brompton Road SW1X 7XL

Harvey Nichols Foodmarket
109–125 Knightsbridge SW1X 7RJ

The Natural Kitchen
77–78 Marylebone High Street
W1U 5JX

Planet Organic
42 Westbourne Grove W2 5SH

Selfridges Food Hall
400 Oxford Street W1A 1AB

Union Market
472 Fulham Road SW6 1BY

Villandry
170 Great Portland Street
W1W 5QB

Whole Foods Market
63-97 Kensington High Street
W8 5SE

Food Markets and Farmers' Markets

Billingsgate Market
Trafalgar Way E14 5ST

Blackheath Farmers' Market
Blackheath Station car park SE3 9LA

Borough Market
8 Southwark Street SE1 1TL

Brick Lane Upmarket
Ely's Yard, The Old Truman Brewery
E1 6QL

Brixton Market
Electric Avenue SW9 8JX

Broadway Market
London Fields E8

Islington Farmers' Market
Chapel Market N1 9PZ

Maltby Street
Maltby Street, Druid Street, Stanworth
Street, The Rope Walk, SE1

Notting Hill Farmers' Market
Car Park Behind Waterstone's,
Kensington Church Street W11 3PB

Portobello Road
Portobello Road W10

Grocers and Farm Shops

A. Gold
42 Brushfield Street E1 6AG

Bumblebee Natural Foods
30_32 Brecknock Road N7 0DD

Chegworth Farm Shop
221 Kensington Church Street W8 7LX

Daylesford Organic
44b Pimlico Road SW1W 8LP

Franklins Farm Shop
155 Lordship Lane SE22 8HX

Highgate Village Fruiterers
3 Highgate High Street N6 5JR

Michanicou Bros
2 Clarendon Road W11 3AA

Partridges
2–5 Duke of York Square SW3 4LY

Yeomans
152 Regents Park Road NW1 8XN

Wine Merchants

Berry Bros & Rudd
3 St. James's Street SW1A 1EG

Bottle Apostle
95 Lauriston Road E9 7HJ

Green & Blue
38 Lordship Lane SE22 8HJ

Jeroboams
20 Davies Street W1K 3DT

Lea & Sandeman
170 Fulham Road SW10 9PR

Philglas & Swiggot
21 Northcote Road SW11 1NG

Planet of the Grapes
9 New Oxford Street WC1A 1BA

The Sampler
266 Upper Street N1 2UQ

Theatre of Wine
75 Trafalgar Road SE10 9TS

Vagabond
18–22 Vanston Place SW6 1AX

Wimbledon Wine Cellar
4 The Boulevard, Imperial Wharf
SW6 2UB

World Food

Athenian Grocery
16a Moscow Road W2 4BT

Green Valley
36–37 Upper Berkeley Street
W1H 5QF

Japan Centre
14–16 Regent Street SW1Y 4PH

Le Maroc
94 Golbourne Road W10 5PS

Loon Fung
42-44 Gerrard Street W1D 5QG

R. Garcia & Sons
246–250 Portobello Road W11 1LL

Taj Stores
112 Brick Lane E1 6RL

Talad Thai
326 Upper Richmond Road SW15 6TL

Turkish Food Centre
89 Ridley Road E8 2NP